Rethinking Services for College Athletes

Arthur Shriberg, Frederick R. Brodzinski, *Editors*

NEW DIRECTIONS FOR STUDENT SERVICES

URSULA DELWORTH and GARY R. HANSON, *Editors-in-Chief*

Number 28, December 1984

Paperback sourcebooks in
The Jossey-Bass Higher Education Series

Jossey-Bass Inc., Publishers
San Francisco • Washington • London

Arthur Shriberg, Frederick R. Brodzinski (Eds.).
Rethinking Services for College Athletes.
New Directions for Student Services, no. 28.
San Francisco: Jossey-Bass, 1984.

New Directions for Student Services Series
Ursula Delworth and Gary R. Hanson, *Editors-in-Chief*

New Directions for Student Services (publication number USPS
449-070) is published quarterly by Jossey-Bass Inc., Publishers.
Second-class postage rates paid at San Francisco, California,
and at additional mailing offices.

Correspondence:
Subscriptions, single-issue orders, change of address notices, undelivered
copies, and other correspondence should be sent to Subscriptions,
Jossey-Bass Inc., Publishers, 433 California Street, San Francisco
California 94104.

Editorial correspondence should be sent to the Editors-in-Chief,
Ursula Delworth, University Counseling Service, Iowa
Memorial Union, University of Iowa, Iowa City, Iowa 52242
or Gary R. Hanson, Office of the Dean of Students,
Student Services Building, Room 101, University of Texas
at Austin, Austin, Texas 78712.

Library of Congress Catalogue Card Number LC 83-82742

International Standard Serial Number ISSN 0164-7970

International Standard Book Number ISBN 87589-789-4

Cover art by Willi Baum
Manufactured in the United States of America

Ordering Information

The paperback sourcebooks listed below are published quarterly and can be ordered either by subscription or single-copy.

Subscriptions cost $35.00 per year for institutions, agencies, and libraries. Individuals can subscribe at the special rate of $25.00 per year *if payment is by personal check.* (Note that the full rate of $35.00 applies if payment is by institutional check, even if the subscription is designated for an individual.) Standing orders are accepted. Subscriptions normally begin with the first of the four sourcebooks in the current publication year of the series. When ordering, please indicate if you prefer your subscription to begin with the first issue of the *coming* year.

Single copies are available at $8.95 when payment accompanies order, and *all single-copy orders under $25.00 must include payment.* (California, New Jersey, New York, and Washington, D.C., residents please include appropriate sales tax.) For billed orders, cost per copy is $8.95 plus postage and handling. (Prices subject to change without notice.)

Bulk orders (ten or more copies) of any individual sourcebook are available at the following discounted prices: 10–49 copies, $8.05 each; 50–100 copies, $7.15 each; over 100 copies, *inquire.* Sales tax and postage and handling charges apply as for single copy orders.

To ensure correct and prompt delivery, all orders must give either the *name of an individual* or an *official purchase order number.* Please submit your order as follows:

Subscriptions: specify series and year subscription is to begin.
Single Copies: specify sourcebook code (such as, SS8) and first two words of title.

Mail orders for United States and Possessions, Latin America, Canada, Japan, Australia, and New Zealand to:
Jossey-Bass Inc., Publishers
433 California Street
San Francisco, California 94104

Mail orders for all other parts of the world to:
Jossey-Bass Limited
28 Banner Street
London EC1Y 8QE

New Directions for Student Services Series
Ursula Delworth and Gary R. Hanson, *Editors-in-Chief*

Contents

Editors' Notes

*"We're different. Athletes are a select group of people who face some unusual
pressures. First of all, we're more visible and more in the spotlight. Then
we put in two and three hours of practice, and still have to study.
Most students just have to balance academics with their social life.
We have to do that and then compete."*
    Todd Blackledge, quarterback, Pennsylvania State University

Student-athletes are different from other students. They have different
needs, pressures, concerns, and demands on their time. Athletes, like
other distinct populations on our campuses — disabled students, returning women, and disadvantaged students, for example — require special
attention. Perhaps more than any other population, they deserve special
services because many of the obstacles and challenges that they face on
the path to graduation are placed there by the institutions that benefit
from their performances. Very few nonathletes could endure the time
demands of a major intercollegiate competition schedule as well as the
psychological and physiological demands of such competition.

College athletes are simultaneously loved and hated, admired
and despised. They are seen as heroes one day and villains the next.
We see them as saviors of the university for the revenue they create and
as pampered, spoiled brats for the benefits they receive. We hear that
large numbers do not graduate, yet research shows their graduation
rate to be higher overall than that of nonathletes. We see them as strong,
mature, and confident individuals, yet we often learn that they cannot
perform in the classroom. Somewhere in the middle of all these images
lies the real student-athlete.

This volume focuses on the college student who happens to be
an athlete. It is extremely important for all of us to remember that the
individual is at the base of the enterprise of intercollegiate athletics,
and how we organize, structure, and operate collegiate sports has a
direct impact on that individual. The character of our institutions is
manifested more in how we treat that individual than in how we perform in the national championships. Recently, much attention has
been focused on the financial elements of intercollegiate athletics and
occasional compromises made in the academic integrity of our institutions. The missing element in those discussions has been the individual
student-athletes.

One cannot understand the milieu of the student-athlete unless one has some knowledge of how intercollegiate athletics are organized, governed, and operated. In Chapter One, James J. Rhatigan provides an insider's view of the demands of intercollegiate competition and poses some logistical questions regarding the personal and academic lives of student-athletes that are indeed very hard to explain. In Chapter Two, Charley Scott unravels the mystery of governance of intercollegiate athletics and clearly reveals who is responsible for enforcing the rules of the game. In Chapter Three, Charlotte West reminds us that *student-athlete* does not mean *male athlete* and that there are some very special problems in women's athletics that need to be addressed. In Chapter Four, Bob Leach and Bob Conners provide insight into the problems of black student-athletes. The general problems of being an intercollegiate athlete are often compounded for black students, yet we tend to forget that they are individuals with all the normal developmental needs of college youth. In Chapter Five, Robert B. Hurley and Robin L. Cunningham approach the delicate subject of providing academic and psychological counseling for student-athletes. Their advocacy of special services for student-athletes is clear. In Chapter Six, Dennis C. Golden tackles quite bravely the role of the chief student affairs officer in supervising college athletes. The challenge of maintaining institutional integrity and a competitive program that addresses the developmental needs of student-athletes is detailed in a candid and sensitive manner by Joseph C. Mihalich, who has experience as an athlete and an administrator. In Chapter Seven, he presents the academician's perspective on collegiate athletics. His research and personal experience on the subject give his comments a poignant perspective. Completing the volume, Arthur Shriberg, Sally Watson, and Frederick R. Brodzinski include an annotated bibliography and a discussion of a variety of resources for additional information. James J. Rhatigan's statement on the rights and responsibilities of student-athletes, which is endorsed by the National Association of Student Personnel Administrators, is included as an appendix. This document should be reviewed on all campuses.

Student-athletes are an important constituency to be served by student affairs professionals. Unfortunately, too many of us know too little about their needs and have little understanding of the challenges inherent in their roles as athletes. Our goal in preparing this publication is to bring to the attention of those in student affairs the need to develop effective services for student-athletes, and to challenge our colleagues to expand their knowledge and involvement in regard to intercollegiate athletics. Intercollegiate athletics affects our institutions, our students, and our work. The responsibility for directing its future lies with each one of us. It is too important an element of higher education to be ignored or to be allowed to be directed or influenced by forces that are not part of our institutions. There is really only one problem with college sports today—too many faculty and administrators—student affairs professionals included—have chosen to be spectators rather than participants in its operation. This situation must change if we are to address the issues presented in this volume.

> Arthur Shriberg
> Frederick R. Brodzinski
> Editors

Arthur Shriberg is vice-president for student development at Xavier University and vice president-elect of the American Association of University Administrators. He chairs a special task force of the American College Personnel Association on the proper role of intercollegiate athletics, and has supervised Division I and II athletic programs at four college campuses.

Frederick R. Brodzinski is dean of students at Ramapo College in New Jersey. He is active in several professional organizations and is a popular speaker at seminars across the country.

Extensive demands placed on student-athletes can be exhausting.
Busy travel schedules, lost study time, and class absences,
as well as emotional and physical stress, can place a heavy
burden on this student group.

Serving Two Masters: The Plight of the College Student-Athlete

James J. Rhatigan

Member schools of the National Collegiate Athletic Association (NCAA) passed legislation during their 1983 convention that has already proven controversial. Steps were taken by the NCAA to better prepare the academically marginal student-athlete for college work. In this chapter, I will comment briefly on these items, and then note why they address only part of the problem the student-athlete faces. My comments will be restricted to the male student-athlete, although women face the same problem.

In the first piece of legislation, the NCAA requires student-athletes to have met a minimum grade point average in core curriculum requirements in high school to better ensure that he can handle his academic responsibilities in college. This thinking is sound in every respect. It will help raise Scholastic Aptitude Test (SAT) and American College Test (ACT) scores because reading ability, not lack of intelligence, has plagued many student-athletes. Some of them assume that they are not going to do well academically, and fail to realize it is skills they lack and not intellectual ability.

Part of the legislation includes a requirement that a student-athlete have a minimum SAT score of 700 or ACT score of 15. These are standard scores and, when broken down into percentages at indi-

A. Shriberg, F. R. Brodzinski (Eds.). *Rethinking Services for College Athletes.* New Directions for Student Services, no. 28. San Francisco: Jossey-Bass, December 1984.

vidual institutions, indicate how an athlete fares when compared with his peers at a given institution.

My opinion is divided somewhat on whether or not to require these minimum scores. On the positive side, the ACT predicts well, at the top and bottom quartiles, the success a student is likely to have in college. On the other hand, these are timed tests with a built-in penalty for the slow reader. The result, then, is not a revelation of how intelligent a student-athlete might be, but how well he can cope with a timed test. The tests, which already cause anxiety for some students, will also be particularly stressful for many student-athletes in the future who will have so much at stake based on the scores.

Perhaps in partial recognition of this fact, the recent NCAA convention passed legislation that would permit institutions to offer athletic scholarships to those who do not meet the minimum standards. The student would be ineligible to play his first year in order to allow him some time to adjust to college. I favor this idea because freshman students are more apt to suffer academically from the pressure of Division I competition.

On the other hand, it may be difficult for freshman athletes to sit out an entire year. The NCAA once had such a rule but reversed it. To use basketball as an example, it is clear that skilled athletes play every day. It is as natural for them as getting up in the morning. Some would argue that the incentive to attend four-year institutions would be reduced if eligibility were curtailed, and that these student-athletes would flock to community colleges across the nation for their first year or two of higher education. Unless community college athletic interests and NCAA Divisions II and III support the plan, Division I schools will be in an even worse bind and will have less time and fewer options to assist the student-athlete.

Part of the problem addressed by the NCAA remains unresolved. It is probably true that students of higher ability can cope better than those at the margin. Yet it is clear that the system we employ is inherently unsatisfactory in many ways. This is particularly true for Division I basketball players. There is little public understanding of what the college athlete experiences. Many people think that the student-athlete is overprivileged, takes easy courses, and coasts through college by doing very little work of substance. Recent media revelations have encouraged that view, but the "dumb jock" is not a new stereotype.

It is worth considering what a collegiate basketball player must contend with in his academic pursuits. It lends credence to the view that the student-athlete is not treated in equal fashion with other students, but differences in treatment do not always favor the student-athlete. In reviewing the second semester (1983) schedules of the Big Ten, Big Eight, and Missouri Valley Conferences in basketball, eight "away" games seem to be the norm. Many other conferences have similar schedules. For the eight "away" games, student-athletes will miss approximately thirteen class days. Most institutions offer approximately seventy-five days of instruction during the semester. This means that the student-athlete is required to be absent from 17.3 percent of classes held that semester, although students may be able to attend some classes on the day of a trip or the day returning from a trip, which reduces the percentage.

At least eighty Division I schools will be involved in post-season competition such as the NCAA tournament and the National Invitational Tournament. Some will know of this only after conferences have scheduled post-season conference play-offs to determine the finalists for the NCAA tournament. (Institutions at other levels have play-offs as well.) Depending on the arrangement, one might add another 2 to 6 percent of required absences on class days for student-athletes at these schools. This commitment is comparable to requiring students to miss 15 to 20 percent of their class work to receive their scholarship, grant, or loan.

In addition, the enforced absences are all early in the spring semester. In calculating the travel schedule of the student-athletes at Division I institutions, eleven weekend days are typically involved in these eight "away" contests. If one considers that the schools are in session approximately fifteen days in January, twenty-eight in February, and thirty in March, seventy-three days are involved. Twenty-four of these days—nearly one third—are taken up by traveling or playing. There are only about fifty class days from January to March. The student-athlete in basketball will miss 26 percent of these classes, minus any classes the athlete can attend before leaving or on returning. For schools in postseason competition, the percentage of required absences on class days is 30 percent from January to March. Faculty expect a study regimen which emphasizes keeping up with assignments and not leaving coursework to intensive last-minute studying; thus it is easy to see the disadvantage faced by student-athletes. Of course, it is possible for students to study while on the road, but this is more difficult than one might think.

Another problem to face is the rigor of extensive travel. Sleeping in a strange bed and eating at unusual hours takes its toll, as does waiting in airports and dealing with misplaced luggage, forgotten textbooks, and so on. Most student-athletes may not be bothered by this, but others can find it difficult. For anyone who has been a student, it is clear that more is involved than merely missing classes. These regular absences are disruptive to the progress of a class and the flow of material which one acquires through regular attendance. The instructor continues from where he or she stopped in the previous session. Notes might be available, but the student-athlete who misses class Monday and returns Tuesday may not have had access to lecture notes before he attends Wednesday. The disruption and frustration this engenders can discourage the student-athlete. Absences tend to encourage more absences.

In addition, the student-athlete might have to arrange to take quizzes or exams he has missed, or to obtain class notes, and may suffer the disadvantage of missing review sessions that some instructors make available to their students as a matter of procedure. In the former case, then, it is valuable time lost; in the latter, it is an opportunity for help that is missed. Some instructors also do not permit make-up exams for any student for any reason. Typically, such instructors offer a number of exams from which the lowest one, two, or three can be dropped. To the extent that student-athletes are required to miss a number of exams, the degree of freedom they have in eliminating low scores is diminished.

Students at some institutions can drop a course by a certain deadline without penalty. If they are receiving federally supported financial aid, they need only complete two thirds of the hours in which they are enrolled in order to be eligible for assistance the following semester. The student-athlete enjoys no such luxury. Students must carry at least twelve hours to participate in intercollegiate competition.

Student-athletes are also hampered by the expenditure of energy. While many students must work hard to earn the money necessary to remain in college, there are very few students who expend themselves the way athletes do. The emotional pressures bearing on the student-athlete are profound. One does not merely go out and play a game. Preparation for each opposing team and the desire to win are both involved. The result can be exhilarating or depressing, but win or lose, the pressure is there. It must be kept in mind that these eighteen- to twenty-one-year-olds play before fans who often expect professional performance. Individual performances are easy to spot, and mistakes are made in front of hundreds or thousands of screaming fans. This distinguishing feature of an athlete's responsibility must be kept in mind. This is not to say, of course, that other performing groups are free of pressure, but the pressure on a Division I student-athlete is severe. Even the job security of the coach they admire and respect may be determined by their performance.

Many students enjoy an extended holiday season. They are able to relax or to work for extra money depending upon their circumstances. There is rarely a break of any length in the schedules of the major basketball schools. There is no opportunity for student-athletes from low-income backgrounds to earn extra money. Many student-athletes would not have sufficient funds for travel home even if there was a break in the schedule.

Basketball players are underrepresented in some academic fields. Is this a question of ability? There is such a phenomenal dedication of energy and commitment to the sport that rigorous academic pursuits may not be possible. The concentration and time necessary for achievement in rigorous curricular ventures is simply too great for many student-athletes. When future engineers, physicians, lawyers, and other professionals do emerge from teams, they may have participated, but in general they are not the first-string or leading team members. The twenty-eight game schedule, the postseason conference play-offs now regularly scheduled, and the postseason tournaments take their academic toll on many student-athletes. It seems a minor miracle that they perform academically as well as they do.

A basis for this extensive schedule is financial profit. It is not true that most schools are generating profit — only a few do — but large sums of money are needed for programs merely to survive. The profit-making sports pay the bills for the non-revenue sports and the salaries and operating expenses of the overall program, and these costs increase annually. If fans across the country had to pay the full bill, it is clear that the programs would not resemble the ones we have today. There would be a cheer in many quarters, of course, over cutting back big-time sports in college, but opposition is strong.

Institutions approach their financial problems in different ways. One solution is to solicit money from private donors. Some institutions use conference affiliation to their advantage. One institution in the Big Eight Conference, in a recent year, took in more money for its football program from television receipts than it did in gate receipts, and did not appear on television. Its share of revenue from four Big Eight schools that were in bowl games produced the funds. The financial packages negotiated in football and basketball by the NCAA now run in the hundreds of millions of dollars, and will continue to grow. The NCAA's ability to continue to control the flow of these funds will no doubt face continuing challenge, with implications for every member school.

It is not too difficult to see how the student-athlete is subordinated in this high-stakes enterprise, and why the cry of exploitation has been raised. It certainly explains the media quest for the quality athlete—

networks are not interested in losing teams. Yet the charge of exploitation is not clear-cut. Where nothing is done for the student-athlete, of course, the issue is clear-cut; but most coaches also want their players to succeed in ways other than athletic competition. The relationship between players and coaches is often so close that one can understand why this would be so, the occasional horror story notwithstanding. Certainly this is true of the campus-at-large.

A Division I colleague's anecdote illustrates this point. A young athlete was intelligent, but was so academically unprepared that a great amount of help had to be extended to him for the young man to academically survive his first year. Through the young man's determination and the assistance of persons at that institution, he eventually graduated. In a relative sense, the student-athlete was probably a comparatively weak graduate at that institution. What impressed and encouraged my colleague was the progress the youngster had made in his schooling.

The young man had come from the inner city. Some of his friends had died before reaching their twenty-first birthdays; others were in jail, in trouble, or doing nothing. It is clear why my colleague felt that this experience was beneficial both to the young man and to the institution. Many institutions might have similar stories to relate. The exploitation we hear of is not in enrolling a student-athlete, but in failing to respond to him throughout his college experience.

With such a dreary picture as I have outlined, one may ask why any student would choose to participate in intercollegiate sports, especially basketball, which cuts across both semesters. It is obvious that these students love to play. The top athlete in basketball knows that he is one of the best not only in this country but throughout the world. For some student-athletes, a part of their personal identity is tied to their role as athletes. It is heady stuff to be written about, talked about, and idolized by fans. For many athletes, the experience is thrilling. It is no wonder that these students treasure their skills and work zealously to improve their athletic talent.

Highly skilled players enjoy the game and fans enjoy watching them. Institutions benefit from the recognition — some have built their schools around athletic achievements, moving then to academic excellence. Television stations and newspapers pay homage to sports at every level. The psychology of sports is deeply embedded and is not going to disappear. Yet all of this is not enough if it occurs at the expense of the education these youths need and deserve.

What can an institution reasonably expect of student-athletes? If we are going to take them away from 26 percent of a semester, as may be the case in basketball, it is just not enough to assume they can catch up in their coursework. How can this be remedied? While insisting on the high school core curriculum, universities should provide their own developmental programs for student-athletes with remedial problems. The number of courses a student-athlete has to take at one time could perhaps be reduced, as is the case among working students, with an institution financing a fifth year or even a sixth year of an education for the student-athlete beyond his years of eligibility. Many schools do this now, but it could become mandatory. Progress can be measured, and no student-athlete should be left to drift from course to course. This charting should be an institutional responsibility, with conference offices looking carefully at the quality of the institution's effort. Even if a student does not graduate, it will still be possible for all concerned parties to feel that the effort was worthwhile.

If a student-athlete comes from an economically deprived home, what provisions can be made for him? Perhaps all grants should be given on the basis of need, raising the ceiling of those in need while restricting dollars for those who are not. (The NCAA has rejected this notion in the past.)

It is not enough to set rules — as much as they are needed — to protect the student-athlete from himself. We need to establish a system that gives student-athletes every chance to succeed, while recognizing an institution's need for the money required to survive, and permitting faithful fans to follow their favorite teams. The debate will continue as to how or whether such a system can be constructed.

James J. Rhatigan is vice-president for student affairs and dean of students at Wichita State University in Wichita, Kansas. He is nationally recognized in student development and has been active in professional associations for many years.

Rules exist at the expense of personal rights to all things and prescribe necessary conditions for orderly conduct of any phase of society.

The Rules of the Game

Charley Scott

Man permits himself to be governed. Easily, existence without government or before government would be chaos. Man has natural tendencies to protect himself and to gain advantage over others. Without common rules of order, they can lead man from constructive occupation into destructive conflict. Hobbes (1651) seems to have seen this more clearly than anyone before him. Others have followed with refinements of this thinking and with a succession of plans for organizing man's activities and relationships.

Today, most men accept and comply with the thought that some ultimate authority provides rules applicable to all members of a common grouping. Through such rules, all may conduct themselves in a spirit of proper expectations. This is particularly important in athletics, where great passions and emotions can come into play.

Several ultimate authorities exist in intercollegiate athletics in the United States of America. Institutions of higher education make choices among these various ultimate authorities according to the mission of each institution for its intercollegiate athletic program. Each one defines for its members a philosophy that forms the base from which all rules stem. One ultimate authority in intercollegiate athletics — the one referred to throughout this chapter — is the National Collegiate Athletic Association (NCAA), which grew out of a crisis that demanded solution through implementation of a governing structure.

A. Shriberg, F. R. Brodzinski (Eds.). *Rethinking Services for College Athletes*. New Directions for Student Services, no. 28. San Francisco: Jossey-Bass, December 1984.

National Collegiate Athletic Association

In the late 1800s and very early 1900s, football resembled a scene of human carnage at each game. Unregulated offenses and defenses resulted in extremely serious injuries to the players. The faculties and administrations of leading institutions discontinued the sport; many others advocated its abolition from the intercollegiate program. Mass formations and gang tackling caused many crippling injuries, and even deaths. The major offense of 1905 was the Flying Wedge — the effects of this formation were disastrous. President Theodore Roosevelt stepped in to attempt to save the game for intercollegiate athletic programs. At a meeting in early December 1905, Roosevelt invited representatives from thirteen institutions to effect reforms in football playing rules. Later that month in New York City, sixty-two colleges and universities agreed to principles for forming the Intercollegiate Athletic Association, in 1910. Its mission in the early years was the definition of rules. Although its purpose has expanded to include other concerns, that mission continues as a major function of the association.

Basic Policy. Today, the NCAA expresses a policy basic for all of its activities (National Collegiate Athletic Association, 1984):

> The competitive athletics programs of the colleges are designed to be a vital part of the educational system. A basic purpose of this association is to maintain intercollegiate athletics as an integral part of the educational program and the athlete as an integral part of the student body and, by so doing, retain a clear line of demarcation between college athletics and professional sports. Legislation governing the conduct of intercollegiate athletics programs of member institutions shall apply to basic athletic issues such as admissions, financial aid, eligibility, and recruiting; member institutions shall be obligated to apply and enforce this legislation, and the enforcement program of the association shall be applied to an institution when it fails to fulfill this obligation [p. 7].

Inherent in this fundamental policy of the NCAA are the political principles attributed to Hobbes, who noted (1651) that legislation becomes necessary as a means of "governing the conduct," and that when government exists, the question of right and wrong arises. The question arises from a legal view (as a result of legislation), not from a moral one, and therein lies a danger. With government, those affected must respect all legislation of the ultimate authority while realizing that the authority can make errors in creating the legislation. Finally, for those who fail to respect all legislation, the ultimate authority must have the power to bring peace. Although the expressions of the political principles caused Hobbes much criticism at the time, his work organized thinking on government as it had not been previously, and served through later ages to provide a philosophical base for governments.

Expanded into the democratic society, conflicts develop in the principles expressed by Hobbes. Basic to a democratic society is the concept that its members can govern themselves. However, following that concept invariably requires the development of an enforcement mechanism. The most effective and palatable system for rules adoption is that one in which the members determine the rules by accepted procedures. The success of that system, however, depends on the willingness of each member to follow the rules adopted within the accepted procedures and on the enforcement system. The crisis in collegiate athletics that resulted in the creation of the organization that became the NCAA reached solution through application of these principles.

The primary membership of the NCAA includes institutions of higher education that meet defined conditions and that subscribe voluntarily to those conditions and the missions of the association. The NCAA maintains a direct involvement of members through participation in development of the association's legislation in a procedure of one vote for each member. One condition of membership in the association is compliance with legislation properly adopted through the defined procedures and participation of the members.

Application of properly adopted NCAA rules to an individual (student-athlete, coach, administrator, and so on) exists entirely within each member institution and its procedures. Accordingly, while the ultimate authority for the member institution is the NCAA — the entire membership in a one member-one vote concept — the ultimate authority for an individual affected in some way by the rules is the member institution. By maintaining membership, the member subscribes to effective application of the rules, including application to individuals within the member's purview.

NCAA Principles

The NCAA expands its fundamental policy into eleven principles that constitute the basis for rules and regulations:

1. The principle of amateurism and student participation relates to rules on pay for play, professional contracts and their relationships, permissible remunerations and expenses, awards, and extra benefits.

2. The principle of institutional control and responsibility defines the obligation of an institution to its intercollegiate athletic program.

3. The principle of sound academic standards provides rules on admission requirements and expected academic conditions.

4. The principles governing financial aid relate to the award of financial aid and to protections for awarded financial aid.

5. The principle governing recruiting establishes the base for control of recruiting practices.

6. The principles of ethical conduct define expectations of university administrators, coaches, and student-athletes in relationship to the NCAA, gambling, professional associations, all-star contests, and consultations.

7. The principle governing competition in postseason and noncollegiate-sponsored contracts restricts such events to conformance with NCAA rules.

8. The principles governing playing and practice seasons establish authorization for defining seasons and for restrictions on association with professional sports contests.

9. The principles governing eligibility of student-athletes defines conditions for eligibility of student-athletes to represent an institution.

10. The principle governing personnel and squad limitations forms a base for rules on the number of employed personnel and the number of student-athletes at an institution.

11. The principle governing football television defines authority of the NCAA in televising football games.

NCAA Rules and Regulations

The NCAA expands those eleven principles into rules and regulations that make possible the operation of a wide variety of athletic programs on a competitive but fair basis. The essential feature of sports competition is fairness, which can come about only when each competitor uses the same rules both on and off the field of competition. Rules arising from principles governing recruiting and eligibility enter considerations with greater frequency, and more intensity, than any others. Both sets of rules impinge directly on student-athletes and depend, therefore, on the integrity of the commitment of a member institution to application.

Recruiting Rules. Recruiting prospective student-athletes constitutes a significant activity in successful major intercollegiate athletic programs. By definition, a prospective student-athlete achieves that status through the action of a staff member of a department of athletics or of a representative of the athletics interest of the member institution to seek the student-athlete's matriculation. The matriculation of a student-athlete at an NCAA member institution must take place within prescribed conditions that define both permissible and unpermissible activities.

Recruiting rules cover offers and inducements, contacts, evaluation periods, publicity, use of funds for recruiting, tryouts, high school all-star games, transportation, visitations, entertainment, precollege expense, sports camps, and coaching schools and clinics. The emphasis of these rules is on fairness in competing for recruitment of a prospective student-athlete for an institution. The intent is that no institution will have an unfair advantage over another in that competition before the student-athlete arrives on a campus to begin a collegiate career. The rules provide quite specific conditions under which recruiting takes place, and attempt to ensure that a prospective student-athlete receives the same treatment from each institution in which the prospective student-athlete may have an interest.

Prohibited financial commitments in recruiting student athletes include:

- Arrangements of employment
- Gifts and tangible items
- Provisions of loans and cash
- Provision of merchandise, services, rentals, purchases, or housing at reduced rates
- Payment of educational expenses before enrollment or after completion of the undergraduate education program
- Transportation costs for relatives and friends for campus visits.

Permitted financial commitments in recruiting student athletes include transportation, meals, accommodations, and limited entertainment expenses for one visit to a campus. The conditions on this one visit include:

- Time is limited to forty-eight hours
- Site is limited to campus of the institution
- Accommodation and meal costs are limited to those comparable to normal student life
- Entertainment is limited to the campus locality with a maximum value and cost handled by a student host
- Transportation costs are limited to specific conditions according to the type used.

Expenses of the visit are defined specifically and are limited to the definitions. Funds used in recruitment efforts come under scrutiny through rules that include full control by the institution.

Contact with a prospective student-athlete can take place under limited conditions. Face-to-face contact with a prospective student-athlete or with parents or guardians can occur off the campus of the institutional representative only as specifically defined in terms of the number of contacts, periods for making contacts, individuals who can make the contacts, and locations for making contacts. In football and basketball, studies of academic standing and playing ability of a prospective student-athlete take place off the campus of the institutional representative during defined periods of time and without personal contact with the prospective student-athlete. Activities designed to cause prospective student-athletes to demonstrate athletic abilities during a recruiting visit may not take place, and physical examinations given only by medical personnel may take place during such a visit.

Eligibility Rules. Eligibility rules define conditions for individual, institutional, and conference eligibility and conditions related to drugs, waivers, protests, and cases of ineligible participation. Individual eligibility relates exclusively to academic considerations both from the standpoint of academic credentials prior to admission and from the standpoint of meaningful enrollment in collegiate courses and progress toward completion of degree requirements. This consideration ensures adherence to the policy of preserving the athletic program as an integral part of the educational program. Admission conditions have a basis of attempting to assure some degree of probable success in the educational program. Academic progress conditions place emphasis on the basic mission of securing a college education as represented by completing requirements for a degree.

To have the opportunity for eligibility for participation in NCAA championships, a student-athlete must:

1. Present acceptable admission credentials from high school records, junior college records, or previous senior college records according to prior experiences of the individual. Conditions for acceptability of the credentials emphasize good academic standing and ethical qualities.
2. Maintain enrollment as a full-time student in a recognized college degree program. The definition of full-time student status rests with the institution's policies but must include specific minimum requirements.
3. Make continuous and satisfactory progress toward completing the requirements of a specific degree program. The minimum progress results in the opportunity for completing the degree requirements in approximately five academic years.

4. Limit participation in intercollegiate athletics to a maximum of four years that may include enrollment in a graduate or professional program or a second baccalaureate program within the allowable time.
5. Meet such other conditions as outlined by the institution represented by the student-athlete or by a conference of which the institution is a member.

The NCAA also prohibits any use of non-prescribed drugs by student-athletes and provides the means for testing for such use.

Waivers of conditions of individual eligibility exist only in a few very limited and specific cases and only by clear decision of the members of the NCAA Council and in one case by the members of the Eligibility Committee. Participation by an ineligible student-athlete results in immediate forfeiture of eligibility for championship participation for one calendar year. Protests of individual eligibility receive attention before and after the period of time from twenty-four hours prior to the beginning of a tournament through the conclusion of the tournament.

Institutional eligibility criteria include:

- Active membership in good standing in a specific NCAA division.
- Eligibility by conference rules of a member of an NCAA conference.
- Application by the institution of all individual eligibility rules.
- Certification annually in writing by the institution's chief executive officer of strict adherence to NCAA rules and policies.

Conference eligibility requirements specify limitations on minimum number of members, minimum number of sports, and methods of determining conference championships. Some conferences adopt NCAA championship individual eligibility conditions as requirements for in-season competition.

Implementation of Rules. Implementation of rules is an expectation from, and an obligation of, an NCAA member institution. Commitment to the expectation and the obligation is the cornerstone for assuring that a member institution places its intercollegiate athletics program within the context of basic NCAA policy. Such commitment comes from institutional control of its athletics program.

Institutional control begins with the tone set by the chief executive officer (CEO) and the governing body of a member institution. The control extends through expectations placed by the CEO on administrators of the athletics programs and through them to the coaches, student-athletes, and others associated with the athletics programs. Through association, other individuals—faculty athletics representatives, student affairs officers, financial officers, admission officers, and so on—have responsibilities to maintain that institutional control. The CEO sets expectations by ensuring that financial stability of the athletics program exists, requiring that total operation of the athletics program complies fully with membership-accepted conditions, developing direct working relationships with the athletics program, and placing accountability as a premier condition of performance on all concerned.

Violations of recruiting rules occur more often than others. They involve improper transportation, improper entertainment, cash payments to prospects, improper housing during visits, improper contacts, and tryouts. Violations usually develop through extra benefits not generally available to other students. Usual extra benefits include money, special loans, and use of automobiles, meals, and clothing. Any one of these constitutes pay for play and results in unfair advantage.

Summary

Intercollegiate athletics in the United States functions within systems of governance just as any other component of society. Basic to the functioning is acceptance by, and commitment of, members to a defined system of governance that is effective and palatable. The NCAA is one system that adopts rules through member participation to assure comparable treatment of members. In the NCAA system, conditions apply to a student-athlete through implementation by a member institution as a part of its obligation to the association. Rules affect a student-athlete in varying ways and to varying extents. The CEO of a member institution has a key role in the NCAA system of governance.

References

Hobbes, T. *De Cive or The Citizen.* New York: Century-Crofts, Inc., 1651.
National Collegiate Athletic Association. *NCAA Manual 1984–1985.* Mission, Kans.: National Collegiate Athletic Association, 1984.

Charley Scott is director of athletics at Mississippi State University. From 1963 to 1984, he served in various academic administration roles at the University of Alabama. Beginning in 1973, he served in leading posts in intercollegiate athletics with the NCAA, the College Football Association, the Southeastern Conference, and the University of Alabama.

*Female athletes have brought a new dimension to collegiate
athletics, but just how lasting and unique that dimension
remains depends largely upon the leadership provided
by women.*

The Female Athlete —
Who Will Direct Her Destiny?

Charlotte West

Throughout history, a parallel has existed between the position of
women in a culture and the extent of their participation in physical
activities. In today's society, the position of women has reached new
and welcomed heights, and, consistent with this elevated position, the
increased participation by girls and women in competitive sports has ex-
ceeded all expectations. In this chapter, two main topics are addressed:
(1) the status of collegiate athletics for women and (2) the administration
of collegiate athletics for women. Each topic includes a brief review of
yesterday, and objective account of today, and a forecast for tomorrow.

The Status of Collegiate Athletics for Women

‛ The growth in participation of girls and women in competitive
sports is a phenomenon that not even the most optimistic among
female athletes would have predicted only a decade ago. A review of
the extent of participation by women in competitive sports prior to the
explosive growth of women's sports in the seventies would lead one to
question whether half of the human race was indeed female. Countless
barriers confronted sportswomen throughout history. For example,

A. Shriberg, F. R. Brodzinski (Eds.). *Rethinking Services for College Athletes.* New Directions
for Student Services, no. 28. San Francisco: Jossey-Bass, December 1984.

when Pierre de Coubertin reestablished the Olympics in 1896, women were barred from participation in keeping with his Victorian ideals. However, in 1900, women participated in tennis and golf in the Olympics held in France, Coubertin's homeland. From 1900 to 1972, 8,500 women participated in the Olympics (Gerber and others, 1974). However, in 1972 alone, 3,000 females experienced the thrill of Olympic sport, and an even greater number participated in the 1984 Summer Olympics in Los Angeles. This surge of participation by women in the Olympics is also occurring on both high school and collegiate levels. Clearly, athletics is no longer the sole domain of the male. It is now a woman's prerogative to participate in and enjoy the benefits of competitive sport, and many women are choosing to become involved.

The growth of women's sports is attributable to several factors, including: (1) increased television coverage of the Olympics, (2) the women's movement, and (3) the enactment of Title IX, which prohibits educational institutions from discriminating on the basis of sex. Each of these factors alone would have stimulated unparalleled growth, but collectively they have caused a growth explosion. The beauty, grace, excitement, and prestige associated with the ultimate experience in international competition, the Olympics, were literally brought into the homes of practically all Americans through the medium of television. This showcasing of women's sports, coupled with the early lack of success of female athletes from the United States, spurred not only Olympic officials, but other American officials as well, to increase funding of and emphasis on grassroots programs for women's sports. The women's movement stressed equal opportunity for all persons regardless of sex or color, and the movement's leaders often used poignant examples depicting the lack of opportunity for women in sport to accentuate the need for change. The dramatic disparities between men's and women's sports programs illustrated the story well.

Perhaps the most important factor contributing to growth was the enactment of Title IX of the Education Amendments of 1972. Once Title IX became law, athletic programs for girls and women grew at an unprecedented rate. In 1970–71, 7 percent (268,591) of all high school athletes were girls. By 1980–81, only ten years later, 35 percent (8,853,789) of all high school athletes were girls. In addition, the number of sports offered for high school girls increased from fourteen in 1970–71 to thirty in 1980–81 (Sports Participation Surveys, 1971 and 1981). In 1971–72, 15.6 percent of all college athletes were women, whereas in 1980–81, only nine years later, this figure had nearly doubled and 30 percent of all collegiate athletes were women. The NCAA News ("'82–'83 A Year of Growth...," 1984) reported that female participation grew 8.9 percent from 1982 to 1983 — an increase in participation from 71,650 to 78,027. It is interesting and important to examine concurrently the participation of male college athletes, which increased 5.85 percent in the same period, and the number of participants to have increased from 167,055 to 176,822.

From the beginning, Title IX opponents decried the legislation and claimed that this government intervention into education would lead to the demise of collegiate athletics for men. These predictions proved to be in grave error, as the funding of men's collegiate sports, the average number of collegiate sports offered for men, and the number of participants in men's collegiate sports all enjoyed substantial increases throughout the years following the enactment of Title IX.

Although fourteen of the nineteen National Collegiate Athletic Association (NCAA) men's sports and nine of the fifteen NCAA women's sports increased in average squad sizes during the 1982–83 school year, evidence is increasing that indicates that the growth of both men's and women's sports is moving toward a state of remission. It is predicted that when future NCAA participation data become available, not only remission but retrenchment in women's programs will have occurred. If retrenchment does occur, this temporary setback should be alleviated by the action of the 1984 NCAA Convention, which mandated a minimum number of sports for women in NCAA institutions. By 1988, Division I schools must offer a minimum of eight sports for women, while Division II schools must offer a minimum of six sports for women.

The average number of sports for women in NCAA schools increased from 6.4 to 6.5 from 1981–82 to 1982–83, while the number of men's sports remained at 9.1. However, if only schools in Division I, the richest and largest schools in the NCAA, are considered, fewer sports for women were actually offered compared to the previous year. This decline reinforced the need for passage of legislation requiring a minimum number of sports for women similar to the existing requirement for men.

Concurrent with increases in the number of sports for women, the number of female participants and events, the number and quality of coaches, uniforms and equipment, the amount and number of athletic scholarship, the amount of media coverage, and other factors have all improved or increased. Such changes are encouraging, and improvement has been truly significant. However, even a dozen years after Title IX became federal law, and even with progress toward equality, discriminatory practices in collegiate sport are by far the rule rather than the exception.

The last place where true equality will be realized is in an athletic setting. In an academic setting, students and professors would not tolerate a 3:00–5:00 P.M. laboratory time for male students while women were assigned to the lab at dinner time, for instance 5:00–7:00 P.M. Amazingly, this practice is common throughout many institutions in athletics. Similarly, students and professors would not tolerate assigning the older editions of a textbook to the female students and distributing the newer editions to the male students. Yet, again, assigning the newer, larger gymnasium to the male athletes and the older, smaller gymnasium to the female athletes for practices and competitions is a common practice in collegiate athletics.

That athletics exists on a college campus primarily because of its educational value to the participant is often overlooked, and the analogy and the propriety of scheduling sports facilities as one would schedule academic facilities is often discarded as irrelevant or invalid. The capability of resisting change and failing to provide equal opportunity for students in all university programs was diminished although not eliminated by the threat of Title IX enforcement. Title IX has been the guillotine in the university courtyard. Although the guillotine has not been used — federal funds have never been withdrawn from a university for failure to comply with Title IX — its very presence has served as a stark reminder to the would-be offender.

Had Title IX remained intact, progress in decreasing discriminatory practices would have continued at a steady rate. However, tampering has occurred, and the Supreme Court ruling in the Grove City case (*Grove City College* v. *Bell,* 1984), which determined that only government-supported programs in the institution, and not the institution itself, are liable, constitutes a serious threat to continued progress in eliminating sex discrimination in athletics. In effect, the guillotine has been removed from the courtyard. As a result, proponents of equal opportunity fear retrenchment in the funding and support of women's athletic programs.

Although retrenchment would not set the status of collegiate athletics for women back to conditions existing in the 1970s, backtracking is likely to occur unless legislation is introduced and satisfactorily passed clarifying the original intent of Congress — that discrimination should not be tolerated in any institutional program or activity directly or indirectly benefiting from federal funds, regardless of what program or activity actually receives the funds. Those who believe that a narrow interpretation of Title IX does not serve as a deterrent to continued growth and funding of women's sports are naive or uninformed. As Sandler (1984, p. 72) aptly states, "Saying that behavior won't change because of the decision is like saying that because we all have free speech now, we don't need the First Amendment anymore. I feel a lot better having the First Amendment. I would also feel a lot better having Title IX back." Sandler reflects the sentiments of most women involved in the administration of athletics, who would also feel a lot better having Title IX back.

The Administration of Collegiate Athletics for Women

The quality of an athletic experience is dependent on the quality of leadership provided. In administration of athletics, leadership can be demonstrated in at least three different ways: (1) participating in a sports governance association that sets rules and regulations for operation of athletic programs; (2) direct coaching of athletes; and (3) administering an athletic program.

Sports Governance Associations. During the initial growth period of women's sports (1971–1981), the Association for Intercollegiate Athletics for Women (AIAW) served as the sports governance association for collegiate women's sports. The AIAW provided an unusual and welcome opportunity for women to assume leadership roles in the conduct of collegiate sports. Although not planned as such, the association became one of the most outstanding affirmative action programs ever in existence. At one time, the AIAW governed sports in junior and community colleges, and in small as well as large colleges. In contrast, the National Junior College Athletic Association (NJCAA), the National Association of Intercollegiate Athletics (NAIA), and the NCAA served as the governance associations for most men's sports programs.

As Title IX and women's sports gained credibility, governance organizations for men implemented women's championships in 1980 as a preliminary measure in assuming ultimate control of women's programs. AIAW leaders opposed such actions because they believed that (1) women student-athletes benefited from an organization devoted exclusively to their needs and interests, (2) men's organizations supported men's interests and actively opposed Title IX, and (3) men's organizations failed to provide comparable leadership and competitive opportunities and also failed to ensure the rights of student-athletes (Grant, 1980).

The final battle consisted of a lawsuit filed by the AIAW against the NCAA for monopolizing intercollegiate athletics. However, the courts ruled in the NCAA's favor, and governance organizations for men succeeded in taking over women's athletics. Since then, women leaders have worked collectively from within the governance organizations to effect change toward increased representation of women and improved regulations for student athletes.

The NJCAA was the first group to assume governance for women's programs, devising a governance structure to provide for equal representation of women. The NAIA installed programs for women in 1980, designating one of their goals as the provision of "equitable representation for women." During the 1984 NAIA Annual Convention, the membership overwhelmingly endorsed a resolution that would guarantee women one-half of all future vacancies on their national executive committee. Arleigh Dodson, faculty representative from Lewis and Clark College and chair of the NAIA Constitution and Bylaw Committee, spoke in behalf of this resolution. Dodson (Crowl, 1984, p. 29) indicated that "there is a special burden on those who oppose the resolution. How else can we live up to our commitment to provide equity for women?" Actions of this type are now readily approved by females involved in the leadership of women's sports. Most women sports administrators opposed attempts by these organizations to assume governance of women's sports. For example, at the 1981 AIAW Delegate Convention, 82 percent of the delegates present voted against the NCAA initiation of governance in championships for women. Yet, a few weeks later, the NCAA assumed governance for women's sports, an action passed by the male-dominated NCAA Convention.

While women have representation on NCAA committees approaching 31 percent, leadership opportunities for women have been reduced from 1,000 to 500 since the NCAA initiated programs for women. Some important NCAA committees—the Select Committee on Athletic Problems and Concerns in Higher Education, for instance—noticeably lack representation by any women directly involved in athletics administration. Factors of this type are viewed as troublesome by females in women's sports leadership.

The assumption that women should formulate policy for women's programs and men should formulate policy for men's programs is presently outdated and has little basis in fact. Either sex is capable of developing a defensible governance system regardless of the athletes' sex. However, as in our patriarchal government, women often bring a unique perspective to issues. Therefore, when women are not elected and when women are selected or appointed in small numbers, the opportunity for novel or different points of view is absent and dimensionality in formulating policy is diminished. Most governance systems in sports are patriarchal and not fully receptive to women with differing points of view. The power bases of the governance systems for athletics are most often controlled by men who in turn tend to select women who align themselves with the male system of governance and are thereby rewarded by it. Quite clearly, a different type of female administrator would be *elected* by women to repreent their prevailing points of view. This problem has not been uncommon for minority groups as they have been mainstreamed into various organizational structures.

Coaches of Women's Sports. In the late 1970s, Holmen and Parkhouse (1980) noted a substantial increase in the number of male coaches in sports in which the AIAW conducted national championships. They predicted that by 1983, half of women's teams would be coached by males.

The accuracy of Holmen and Parkhouse's prediction as shown in data compiled by Acosta and Carpenter (1984) is astounding. Acosta and Carpenter have continued a long-term study in which they examined percentages of men and women coaching women's teams. In 1984, 53.8 percent of women's teams were coached by men, closely paralleling earlier predictions, and five of the ten most popular NCAA sports for women have more male coaches than female coaches. Increasing percentages of male coaches reflect decreasing opportunities for female coaches, since very few females have been selected to coach all-male teams.

Analyses of the perceptions of persons involved in the conduct of sport that address this declining opportunity for women differ on the basis of the respondent's sex. Male respondents attribute the decline to women—specific explanations include: (1) a lack of qualified women, (2) an unwillingness of women to recruit and travel, and (3) a failure of women to apply for positions. Women, however, attribute the decline to: (1) the strength of the old boys network, (2) a lack of strength in the women's network, and (3) unconscious discrimination by those who hire. Regardless of the perceived causes, as sports participation opportunities for female athletes have increased significantly, opportunities for female coaches have decreased significantly.

Administration of Women's Athletic Programs. Acosta and Carpenter have also studied the administrative structure of intercollegiate athletic programs for women in detail. Prior to 1972, only 6 percent of Division I women's athletic programs were merged with the men's programs. By 1979, 64 percent were combined, and the percentages continue to increase. Virtually all combined programs have a male as the director of athletics. To date, there is but one exception to this practice in Division I athletic programs.

Regardless of the organizational structure of athletics, 86.5 percent of women's programs have a male administrator. Surprisingly, 38 percent of the institutions have no women at all involved in the administration of athletics. Again, although the participation rates of women athletes continue to increase, regardless of the area of leadership surveyed—sports governance, coaching, or administration—leadership roles for women continue to decrease. If the full value of the new and unique perspective of women is to be realized, this trend must be reversed.

Concluding Remarks

Collegiate athletic programs for women are characterized by some unique differences when compared to men's programs. In addition, various physical, psychological, and academic profiles of male and female athletes differ. The dissimilar stages of development of men's and women's programs partially account for some of these differences. Physical and physiological differences between the sexes account partially, as does the distinctiveness of athletes involved. Further, characteristics and philosophies of leaders in the programs also account partially for some differences. Some differences are simple in nature and can be readily explained. Other distinctions are extremely complex and are undoubtedly a function of multiple factors. Several differences are presented without attempting to analyze or to explain their causes.

The concept of a student-athlete as a student first and an athlete second has long been endorsed by athletic administrators. This concept is far more evident in women's athletic programs than in those for men. Female athletes tend to earn higher grade point averages than their male counterparts and the general student population. Female athletes also have higher retention rates and graduation rates than their male counterparts, and, again, higher than the general student population. How long these differences will exist is a timely question, and the answer would undoubtedly reflect the perceived causes of the differences.

Female athletes face unique problems because of their sex. For example, as female athletes train in a more rigorous manner, they are increasingly likely to experience amenorrhea, a temporary cessation of the menstrual cycle. Until recently, this physical manifestation of serious training deterred some female athletes from continued training and participation. However, recent research with highly trained athletes has provided essential knowledge about amenorrhea which has allayed unwarranted fears about the permanence and lasting effects of the condition. Female athletes are generally a health-conscious group. Because of concern over possible negative side-effects of many popular methods of birth control, athletes frequently do not employ routine birth control methods. Whether this is a factor or not, the number of pregnancies among college athletes is increasing. Once pregnant, the athlete is often faced with serious moral and physical dilemmas that have serious ramifications for her athletic and academic performances.

One of the most striking differences between male and female athletes involves the incidence of eating disorders. The prevalence of eating disorders among female athletes is shockingly high. Whether this type of disorder among females is more physically or emotionally based is a matter still under study. Many female athletes prefer to resolve very personal and physical problems with the help of a female mentor; for others, the sex of the counselor/friend is irrelevant.

Another specific problem facing female athletes is the potential for experiencing role conflict. The stereotypic and dichotomous view of acceptable feminine behavior and successful athletic behavior constitutes a source of dissonance for the female athlete. Appropriate and inappropriate behavior by sex is learned at a very early age, and one of the most salient differences in male and female role expectations involves sports participation. The contradiction in dual roles between being an athlete and being a woman has resulted in various modes of behavior from overcompensation manifested by apologetic behavior and ultra-feminine dress to withdrawal from participation. Since role conflict is externally imposed upon the female athlete rather than internally derived, the potential for conflict will be reduced accordingly as society refines and accepts an increasingly broader and humanistic view of sex-role behaviors (Anthrop and Allison, 1983).

Aside from role conflict, society has contributed to another difference in men's and women's athletic programs — the relative emphases placed on educational and financial objectives. The public perception of success and ensuing pressures placed on individuals involved in men's athletics have caused many educational objectives to be usurped by financial and other objectives and for athletics to be treated more as a business venture than an educational endeavor. Sports can be educational in nature and still be financially lucrative, but the antithetical challenge to do both simultaneously is extremely difficult.

The overemphasis on winning not only pervades professional and intercollegiate athletics, but high school and recreational athletics as well. The gauge for athletic success is more frequently the win-loss record rather than how well the game was played or whether positive values accrued from athletic participation. How often are coaches retained because the athletes under their direction did well academically, graduated in impressive numbers, displayed good sportsmanship, learned to forsake individual goals for the good of the team, learned to lose with dignity, and attained other important objectives? More often than not, coaches are retained because of their number of wins. As intercollegiate athletics for women becomes more publicly visible, the preoccupation with winning at the expense of educational values will be one of the greatest problems to counter. This is a societal as well as an institutional problem that needs the immediate and careful attention of the best available leadership. Hopefully, women will not be excluded from the decision-making process.

If the number of female leaders in athletics continues to decrease, women's athletic programs will mirror to an even greater degree the image of men's programs and forfeit those unique areas which are presently superior in women's programs. In order to ensure the most effective and educationally sound experience for all students involved in athletics, leadership should involve a cross-section from the population at large. Role models of each sex and race are important in the healthy development of all persons. The destiny of the female athlete, and, similarly, the destiny of the male athlete, should be plotted and guided by women as well as by men. Only then will the destiny show promise.

References

Acosta, R. V., and Carpenter, L. J. *Changing Status of Women in Intercollegiate Athletics.* Brooklyn: Department of Physical Education, Brooklyn College of the City University of New York, 1984.

Anthrop, J., and Allison, M. "Role Conflict and the High School Female Athlete." *Research Quarterly,* 1983, *54* (2), 104–111.

Crowl, J. A. "NAIA to Reserve Leadership Positions for Women; 'Eligibility Fee' Rejected." *Chronicle of Higher Education,* March 28, 1984.

"'82–'83 A Year of Growth in Men's, Women's Sports." *NCAA News,* February 29, 1984, p. 1 and p. 20.

Gerber, E., Felshin, J., Berlin, P., and Wyrick, W. *The American Women in Sport.* Reading, Mass.: Addison-Wesley, 1974.

Grant, C. *AIAW Responses to Questions Relating to 1980 NCAA/NAIA Proposals for Championships for Women.* Unpublished memorandum, 1980.

Grove City College v. *Bell,* 104 S. Ct. (1984).

Holmen, M., and Parkhouse, B. "Report Reveals Trends in Women's Athletics." *NAGWS News,* 1980, *9* (4), 3.

Sandler, B. R. "The Quiet Revolution on Campus: How Sex Discrimination Has Changed." *Chronicle of Higher Education,* February 29, 1984, p. 72.

Charlotte West is professor of physical education and director of intercollegiate athletics for women at Southern Illinois University. She has served as president of the Association for Intercollegiate Athletics for Women, and as a member of the United States Olympic Committee. She is now serving on the Executive Committee of the National Association for Collegiate Directors of Athletics.

For predominantly white colleges and universities that enroll
black student-athletes, to continue to ignore the special needs
of these students will elevate what many already call a national
disgrace to tragic proportions.

Pygmalion on the Gridiron: The Black Student-Athlete in a White University

Bob Leach
Bob Conners

Our task in this chapter is to engage in a forthright discussion of the special needs of black student-athletes who enroll at predominantly white colleges and universities, and to discuss the role of the student affairs administrator in influencing institutional policy to meet these needs. In so doing, we will inevitably repeat some of what the reader has encountered earlier in this volume. Because this issue receives much public attention and since there are larger ethical issues involved, we risk redundancy to imbue in the reader a sense of urgency needed to confront this problem.

Before there can be any meaningful understanding of the special circumstances of the black student-athlete at the predominantly white institution of higher education, one must ask what it is to be black and athletically talented in America. Black athletes, like students from other nonwhite subcultures, usually experience years of systematic degradation. Nowhere is this more apparent than in America's public schools (Kozol, 1967; Rosenthal, 1968).

A. Shriberg, F. R. Brodzinski (Eds.). *Rethinking Services for College Athletes.* New Directions
for Student Services, no. 28. San Francisco: Jossey-Bass, December 1984.

For many talented young black athletes, the process of degradation begins long before they arrive on the university campus. Their problems begin when they discover that they are more agile and better coordinated than their peers. Athletic success becomes a powerful lure that draws them from less rewarding experiences in the classroom. Many discover that when they perform especially well on the playing field, little is expected of them off the field, either academically or socially. These unhealthy intellectual and social patterns are gradually incorporated into the self-concept (Haughey, 1982). By the time many star black athletes complete high school, so little has been expected of them academically that they have come to expect as little of themselves.

As if the academic self-concept of many a black athlete is not sufficiently impaired by anti-academic and anti-intellectual forces, there is a compelling and conspicuous absence of alternative professional role models in television and other popular media. Lacking black counterparts to such positive television character role models as Perry Mason or Marcus Welby, the most pervasive black model for success — indeed, other than black entertainers, the only consistent model for success — is the professional black athlete (Edwards, 1983). The image of a culture preoccupied with sports is beamed into the homes and the imaginations of millions of black youth. The message conveyed to them is, "This is your ticket." Thousands of hours of professional competition aired each year mask the the fact that "fewer than 2,400 black Americans can be said to be making a living in professional athletics today" (Edwards, 1983, p. 33). (See Bandura, 1971a, 1971b, for a discussion of the power of role-modeling through television.)

For the talented young black athlete, a career in professional sports represents the path to the top. College is seen by many as the athletic farm system where one can be noticed by professional scouts. For the poorly prepared student-athlete, higher education becomes a means to this end.

Considering the power of dominant white cultural forces that impel the talented black athlete toward dreams of a professional career, it is not surprising that "the black family and the black community tend to reward athletic achievement much more than any other activity" (Edwards, 1983, p. 32). Particularly for the poor, educational achievement is likely to be unappreciated and go unrewarded. In a home where basic survival concerns are paramount, a curious mind may even be viewed as a nuisance.

So, even before entering a predominantly white college or university, the black student-athlete often brings with him or her an overwhelming array of pressures, and for many of these black athletes, whether or not they are prepared for higher education, they have not been prepared for the white culture in which they are about to compete. Many black athletes are first-generation college students. Even if their parents are college graduates, most were not athletes, nor were they likely to attend predominantly white institutions. Their counsel to sons and daughters who are athletes may have little validity. So, not only is it a new ball game, it is a game with new rules.

A Breach of Contract

For the past two decades contracts have been struck between black athletes and institutions of higher education — an education in exchange for athletic performance (Edwards, 1983). The accomplishments of black athletes in the major collegiate revenue-earning sports speak for themselves. However, the record of universities on behalf of black student-athletes suggests that the label *student-athlete* (not *athlete-student*) was coined by design. Moving quickly to the bottom line, we find that only 25 to 35 percent of black student-athletes who attempt higher education graduate with a bachelor's degree (Edwards, 1983). What happens to many of those who do not make it is what some have called a "national disgrace" (Underwood, 1980).

Wittmer and others (1981) and other writers chronicle a litany of abuses that lend credence to Underwood's assessment (1980). For example, grade scandals rocked the Pacific 10 conference in the late seventies ("Sport Editorial," 1980) and one major western school has graduated no black basketball players and only sixteen black football players since 1970 (Warfield, 1984). There have been numerous news stories of black college basketball players who have graduated from universities with limited or no ability to read and write (CBS, *Sixty Minutes,* 1980, PBS, *Blacks in Sport,* 1984). Anecdotal testimonies of other abuses of black student-athletes add up to cause one to wonder how widespread they are. Apparently, the National Collegiate Athletic Association wonders also, since in 1983–84 it doubled the size of its investigative division to handle an upsurge in violations.

Underwood (1980) creates a particularly damning scenario for many academically underprepared students:

> From the moment the student athlete sets foot on campus, the name of the game is "majoring in eligibility," and it is a vulgar, callous, shameful, cynical, and perfectly legal exploitation of the system *by and for* (emphasis ours) the American college athlete. The formal term for it is normal progress toward a degree.

But the NCAA's definition of progress won't be found in any dictionary; for one thing, progress in the student-athlete lexicon can mean no progress at all [p. 43].

Wittmer and others (1981) conclude that majoring in eligibility seems to be especially true for the black athlete when "at the end of four years of college courses the athlete is no closer to a B.S. or B.A. degree than a lower-division college student" (p. 53).

Furthermore, the mentality of majoring in eligibility transforms the 4.0 grading system to a 2.0 grading system in which the student strives to achieve just enough to get by academically. Meanwhile, in the face of growing numbers of limited-access academic programs at many institutions (for instance, degree programs requiring a higher-than-average grade point to enter a certain academic major), many student-athletes find themselves forced into "majors generally held in low repute" (Edwards, 1983). Edwards (1983) estimates that 75 percent of the minority of black student-athletes who graduate receive degrees in "physical education or in majors created specifically for the athlete" (p. 32). "With limited job qualifications," he continues, "the black athlete who blindly sets out today to fill the shoes of Dr. J., Reggie J., Magic J., Kareem Abdul J., or O.J. may well end up with no J — no job that he is qualified to do in our modern, technologically sophisticated society" (p. 33).

Up to this point we have depicted the black student-athlete as a victim of ruthless social forces, and as someone having no free will. But Underwood (1980) suggests that "exploitation of the system" is done "by and for" the student-athlete. Many student athletes choose to major in eligibility. Some hope to hang on long enough to be noticed by a professional scout for that long shot at professional stardom. Others, hampered by years of academic apathy, even antipathy, choose the major in eligibility to avoid further damage to an already weakened academic self-concept. (Haughey, 1982, discusses avoidance of academic challenge as a common trait of the academically underprepared student.) Still others, finding themselves in full-blown academic, social, and athletic competition with white students for the first time, retreat down the path of least resistance, uncertain of their identity in a world they neither understand nor trust.

While certainly not every black student-athlete is an academic tragedy, one must take seriously the Darwinian world our colleges and universities present to them. Seventeen-, eighteen- and nineteen-year-old youth are expected to demonstrate clarity of purpose and exercise a degree of self-discipline that would make Nietszche's superman envious.

We must allow that behind an apparent exercise of free will is a process of intensive and lifelong cultural conditioning that narrows a black athlete's ability to perceive other paths of opportunity.

If the picture we have painted has any validity, the black student athlete in particular is the loser. So who are the winners? At one Southern institution that graduates an average of only 28 percent of its football players—black and white—$1.5 million was spent in 1982–83 on scholarships and other direct services for its student-athletes. For the same period, revenue from booster organizations and ticket sales alone totalled $5 million.

Big-time intercollegiate programs do incur huge operating expenses beyond the cost of direct support for student-athletes, but the issue is one of perspective. One wonders whether student-athletes are being adequately compensated for their contributions when the annual salary of the head football coach (including outside perks) at some institutions approaches the total annual outlay for all student athletic scholarships.

Casting the treatment of student-athletes in this light should be shocking to any conscientious constituent of the academic community. The worst-case scenario is one of moral neglect in which the relationship between the historically white institution and its black athletes in particular can best be described as a system of exploitation and parasitism. A parasite, according to *Webster's New Collegiate Dictionary* (Wolfe and others, 1981, p. 825), is something that is "in dependence on something else for existence or support without making a useful, adequate return." We submit that the pressures to compete in big-time intercollegiate athletics are forcing institutions toward an increasingly parasitic posture with black student-athletes, and, to an increasing degree, with student-athletes in general. Viewing the black student-athlete from this perspective suggests the need for a more comprehensive role for the student affairs administrator.

Treating the Elusive Patient

The tone of righteous indignation that characterizes the first pages of this chapter is intentional, though it is not our intent to be vindictive or to isolate a particular institution or constituency for criticism. We have rather sought only to echo the sense of urgency that one finds throughout the professional and popular literature on this topic. As an issue, the plight of the black student-athlete is relatively new, and literature on the subject is meager. In professional journals, one can find articles describing revolutionary programs for student-athletes in career education, values clarification, comprehensive academic advisement, and, of course, stress management. Generally, these are courses designed to teach student-athletes how to cope with the pressures of their special situation. To justify their interventions, some of these authors go to great pains to chronicle in greater detail than we have here the myriad of abuses of the student-athlete (for instance, Wittmer and others, 1981).

The common and disturbing discovery is that after damning the collegiate apparatus as parasitic and unprincipled, most authors then describe programs to assimilate the student-athlete into the perverse order they have so convincingly decried. In relation to the real problem, the suggestion of these well-intentioned gestures can be compared with the fable "The Three Blind Men and the Elephant." One man, grasping the trunk of the elephant, calls it a snake; the second, embracing a leg, proclaims it to be a tree trunk; and the third, swinging from its tail, calls it a vine — they cannot or will not see the elephant.

Dealing with something as big as an elephant, the student affairs administrator faces a serious problem. Treatment is analogous with that of the family therapist who is asked to treat the problem child in a family. The problem child is labeled the *identified patient*. This implies that there are unidentified patients. The skilled therapist, instead of treating only the identified patient, examines how the family and the child collaborate to create the problem in the child, and, more important, how each member avoids confronting substantive inter- and intrapersonal issues of their own by focusing on the problems of the child. In this broader perspective, the whole family becomes the patient. Large systems such as colleges and universities operate in similar ways.

But before one can administer treatments one has to know the territory. Before embarking on a discussion of specific measures to assist the black student-athlete, we must look at the problem components and how they unwittingly conspire to maintain and advance the status quo. Discovering what these components are and understanding how they operate is essential to the development of any lasting solution to the problems faced by black student-athletes on predominantly white campuses.

On every college campus the student-athlete walks a thin line between admiration and resentment by the university community. Although these are opposite emotions, often they are expressed within the same constituencies. Fellow students, for instance, turn out by the thousands to support football and basketball teams and take pride in athletic victories. These same students coin condescending labels for courses that are considered less than challenging, such as "Rocks for Jocks" or "Football Physics." Some students joke that the term *athletic scholarship* is a contradiction in terms. Many believe that athletic stipends deplete the pool of dollars available for academic scholarships. Still others see luxurious housing and free meals for scholarship athletes as undue pampering. The resentment that many in the student body have for the student-athlete is born largely of ignorance, and serves to isolate the scholarship athlete from the mainstream.

In a conversation with one of the authors, a black football player at a predominantly white Southern institution expressed his frustration with both black and white students, who accused him of "having the life." Everything was taken care of for him, they claimed. He received free meals, his tuition and books were paid for him, he got a free roof over his head, he received spending money, and even his classes were selected for him. Shaking his head in frustration, he said:

> They think it's easy! They don't know about the daily routine during the season, the control of practically every minute of my life from Sunday night study hall until the game is over on Saturday night. They don't know about getting up at 6:30 in the morning to lift weights; then going to classes all morning; the team meetings after lunch, viewing films, taping up and dressing out; then, two or more hours of practice; then, you clean up and usually go home to catch a nap until supper; then it's two hours of study hall and at 10 o'clock at night I'm free. But most of the time I'm too tired to do anything but watch TV. You can forget the books. Some of them (other students) just go to class. They don't even work. Others shelve books in the library for two hours a day or sit in an office and type and think they're "putting out." My schedule would kill them! They just don't know!

This frustrated student put his finger on the real obstacle to substantive change on behalf of the student athlete — widespread ignorance of the demands that modern intercollegiate competition makes on today's student-athlete.

The resentment that the student-athlete probably feels most poignantly comes from faculty. Faculty resentment tends to be the result of growing tension between big-time college athletic programs and the basic academic values that undergird institutions of higher education. Many faculty see these two camps in diametric opposition to one another. Each views the other with suspicion and disdain.

Recently, at one institution whose athletic program and faculty-student makeup is typical of the sixty-three member institutions of the

College Football Association, over 500 faculty were queried about their attitudes toward student-athletes and intercollegiate athletics in general. In response to one item, 84 percent ($n = 290$) of the 347 respondents who expressed an opinion believed athletic administrators on that campus to be "uncommitted" (19.6 percent) or "only marginally committed" (65.4 percent) to ensuring quality education for student-athletes (President's Committee on the Student Athlete, 1984b). Over half (50.8 percent) of these opinionated faculty cited poor academic performance of student-athletes and the conviction that athletic program administrators view sport as more important than academics.

One faculty member's response in a follow-up interview was typical. "Our research library is going down the drain and we spend millions on the jocks. Meanwhile, the library has cancelled a subscription to one of the most prestigious journals in my field." In fact, the athletic program at his institution is a financially self-supporting enterprise and had recently donated $100,000 to the beleaguered university library. This faculty member's perception was not accurate, but his frustration was real.

It appears that most faculty are not only ignorant of the relationship between athletic programs and the rest of the university but also of the athletic demands placed on the individual student-athlete. In the same faculty survey, although more than 80 percent ($n = 408$) of the respondents claimed to be "very informed" or "somewhat informed" about intercollegiate athletics, when pressed on specifics in follow-up items 67 percent were "not at all informed" about practice schedules, 47 percent were "not at all informed" about recruiting practices, 46 percent were "not at all informed" about athletic scholarships, and 36 percent were neither informed about academic support services available to student-athletes, nor about the role of the student-athlete's academic advisers.

A confidential survey of most student-athletes at the same institution corroborated these findings. When asked to respond to the statement, "My profesors are sensitive to my athletic pressures," only one-quarter (24.4 percent) of 387 respondents could agree; 41.8 percent disagreed, and 33.5 percent were undecided. A majority of male and female black student-athletes in all sports but one (men's track and field) disagreed with this statement, and white respondents tended to be undecided. Even more alarming, however, were responses to the item, "I believe that some of my professors have discriminated against me in grading practices because I am a student-athlete." More than one-third (139) of 359 respondents agreed with this statement, while 42 percent disagreed and 18.4 percent were undecided. Interestingly, an almost equal percentage of black and white football players agreed (blacks, 53.6 percent, whites, 54.1 percent) that some faculty were discriminating against them in assigning grades.

Whether or not there is truth behind this sentiment, it is the perception of these athletes that faculty discriminate against them that is most disturbing. In fact, a review of final grades in more than 110,000 course sections at this university during a five-year period (1977–82) yielded the names of only thirteen faculty members who graded student-athletes differently from other students in two or more sections. Of these thirteen, only one displayed a pattern of unusual grading that was statistically significant (President's Committee on the Student Athlete, 1984c).

The Student Affairs Administrator:
Defrocked in the Land of the Trinity

Could it be that so many student-athletes perceive faculty to be negative or, at best, indifferent towards them as students? If so, part of the reason may be the general skepticism and ignorance of faculty about modern intercollegiate athletics. But faculty indifference toward student development in general may represent an even greater obstacle to the student affairs administrator. This indifference springs from basic values of higher education to which most faculty subscribe and which figure prominently in the mission statements of most large research-oriented institutions. We shall refer to these values as the *holy trinity:* academic research, teaching (graduate education), and service.

In 1967, a fascinating survey of faculty and administrators at sixty-eight U.S. colleges and universities revealed some interesting facts about the relative importance of what we call *student development* (Gross, 1977). Approximately 9,000 administrators and 7,000 faculty were asked to assign relative importance to forty-seven institutional goals. Eighteen of these goals made direct reference to students — for instance, "Produce a well-rounded student, that is, one whose physical, social, moral, intellectual, and esthetic potentialities have all been cultivated" (p. 262). In short, the survey uncovered "a singular scarcity of any emphasis on goals that have anything to do with students." Gross (1977) concludes:

> In general, then, students as a group are not felt to be particularly important, nor is there strong feeling that the situation in that respect is different from what it ought to be. . . . Nor is there any evidence, either in what goals are or what they should be, to

suggest that it is an important goal of the university to prepare a student for a useful career, to assist him in upward mobility, to assist him to be a good consumer, or to become a good citizen [p. 273].

There are two obvious problems in citing this research as evidence of prevailing faculty attitudes: First, a survey conducted in 1967 cannot be regarded as current, and second, many more administrators than faculty were sampled. However, these findings do chronicle a traditional attitude in modern higher education, and they are not incongruous with the holy trinity mission statements which govern many modern institutions. Student affairs administrators need only rely on their own intuition and observations to accept or reject this argument. Comparison of their own budgets to those of other constituencies in the university may also be persuasive. (For instance, the annual student affairs budget of one former executive of the National Association of Personnel Administrators represents less than 1 percent of his institution's total annual budget.)

Recently, in a conversation with one of the authors, one prominent faculty member summarized a common faculty perception of the role of student affairs. "Student affairs," he said, "is the hardware of the institution, and it is secondary to academic considerations." It would seem that there is little room in the holy trinity for undergraduate student development. Indeed, in the national survey cited above (Gross, 1977), faculty and administrators placed forty-fourth of forty-seven the goal of "emphasizing undergraduate instruction even at the expense of the graduate program" (p. 271). This is not to imply that faculty do not care about the undergraduate student, but that relative to the traditional mission of the large research institution, the undergraduate student occupies a decidedly secondary position.

Consider, then, the position of the student-athlete who represents educational anti-matter in the minds of many academicians. Consider further the black student athlete, particularly the underprepared student who must contend with racial as well as athletic stereotyping. The student affairs administrator cannot afford to ignore these elements in any serious attempt to intervene on behalf of the black student-athlete.

Finally, in our list of constituencies that direct the lives of student-athletes, we have, as Reggie Jackson once said, the "straw that stirs the drink" — the athletic community. "Coaches," as Edwards (1984) puts it, "are nice guys, generally. But, they've got to win or they're gone. Coaching is a high-paying job with low job security." Some coaches succumb to the pressure and resort to forms of cheating such as illegal recruiting, financial inducements, or grade fixing. Others play fairly, only to have a few rich alumni place the institution in jeopardy by purchasing a new car for a young, gifted prospect, or by arranging for other alumni and boosters to make extensive purchases from Dad's struggling Acme Widget Company at the time of the date for signing recruits to their athletic contracts with the institution. These behaviors are exceptions to the rule, but the growing number of infractions reveals the pressure that coaches experience from the community, especially from athletic booster organizations.

It would be naive to suppose that these pressures are not communicated to the players, especially to those who play the revenue-earning sports. Typically, football and basketball are the money earners, and it is in these sports where most black athletes are concentrated. In such an environment, academic achievement beyond normal progress can readily take a back seat to winning. One institutional survey of football and basketball corroborated this sentiment. When asked to respond to the statement, "My coaches are sensitive to my academic pressures," almost 52 percent of the school's football and basketball players disagreed. Among blacks the figure was closer to 60 percent (President's Committee on the Student Athlete, 1984a).

For many institutions that participate in Division I NCAA sports, the environment is characterized by internecine tension. At its worst it is a world of suspicion where faculty question the motives of athletic administrators, and athletic administrators see faculty as naive and ignorant of the realities of big-time intercollegiate athletics. Athletes are at once admired, resented, and envied by their student peers. As "dumb jocks" they are an "insult" to academic integrity. Their coaches, ignorant of or indifferent to the academic responsibilities of student-athletes, make extreme demands.

To return to our analogy of the problem family, our therapist knows that treating only the identified patient (the black student-athlete) is ultimately fruitless if one does not treat the patient's context (the university family) where persistent patterns will most likely render any changes in the patient's behavior temporary. In other words, we can produce an assertive, unstressed, goal-oriented, and values-clarified student-athlete in a vacuum, but the persistence of these changes is questionable unless we alter the student-athlete's environment. This is especially true for the black student-athletes, for whom the ways of the predominantly white university culture are already perplexing. Current efforts to help black student-athletes cope are well-intentioned and within themselves fundamentally sound, but the student affairs administrator can enhance prospects for success by attempting systems-level interventions on behalf of the black student-athlete.

Strategies for Influencing Institutional Policy
on Behalf of the Black Student-Athlete

In any organization, the change agent is constrained by the system in which he or she operates. One must know the territory to determine the means through which and the degree to which change is possible. To illustrate the problem, we refer to an urgent question that is being asked by the brightest minds in the change business today. "How many student affairs professionals does it take to change a light bulb?" The answer is, of course, unknown, since the light bulb first has to want to be changed. Similarly, it is axiomatic that a system changes when its constituents become disenchanted with the status quo, and therefore desire change. But change must be more than movement away from an unsatisfactory status quo, which is merely avoidance of the problem. Lasting positive change is characterized by movement toward a more positive set of goals and aspirations. In our treatment of the black student-athlete, these goals should include a higher quality of life for the student-athlete that embodies the principles associated with centers of higher learning. This form of change is growth.

Many change strategies can be employed to accomplish this growth. It would behoove student affairs administrators to become familiar, if they are not already, with models of institutional change, and to select one that is appropriate to their institution (see Smith and others, 1981). For our illustration we will use the basic classic procedure described by Lewin (1948), from which all modern organizational change and development models proceed.

Lewin proposed three basic stages of deliberate change: Stage I, unfreezing the status quo; Stage II, change or movement; and Stage III, refreezing, or the integration of change into the order. Unfreezing the status quo suggests a shake-up of things as they are and an examination of the problems from perspectives representative of the institution's constituents. At this stage, identified problems are investigated to determine the need, if any, for change. Stage II, the change stage, is self-explanatory and will be dealt with in the context of addressing the needs of the black student-athlete later in this chapter. Finally, Stage III, refreezing, refers to institutionalizing consensual change.

In any social system, unfreezing the status quo usually results in an awareness of the need for change. Though the needs of the black student-athlete are real, there are many competing interest groups. The chorus of demands for change can become overwhelming. Most institutions now recognize the special needs of disabled students, returning women, military veterans, single-parent students, commut-

ing students, international students, and racial minorities in gen.
Yet many of us at predominantly white institutions have been blind
by the glory of the Big Game each Saturday. We have neglected our
responsibility to communicate to others that a toll is being exacted from
student-athletes—a physical, social, and academic toll. They pay this
toll so that we can cheer on Saturday night.

The toll on some black student-athletes is too great, and there
are resultant problems. Unfortunate incidents involving student-athletes
force this reality into our consciousness and challenge our complacency.
Following a series of such incidents involving black student-athletes at
his institution, one of the authors spearheaded an effort to establish a
university-wide committee to investigate the status of the student-athlete.
The case was made that these incidents may be symptomatic of a larger
problem. The committee quickly discovered institutional problems in
the treatment of student-athletes. The committee moved beyond the
individual to the system in its investigation. The thaw of the status quo
had begun (see President's Committee on the Student Athlete, 1984c).

There are certain principles of unfreezing the status quo to
which the student affairs administrator must adhere in order to enhance
successful policy making. To give a problem legitimacy, the investi-
gator or investigating body must have credibility within the community. Traditionally, for reasons we have discussed, student affairs
administrators have not been in a position to shape the destinies of
institutions of higher education. Recognizing this reality, it is important that investigative efforts be initiated and maintained by the institution's chief executive officer (Smith and others, 1981).

Investigative teams or committees are best suited to the work.
Membership should be representative of the university community. It
is vital that members of the problem constituency be included. For
instance, members of the athletic administration and booster organizations, the prime movers in the nonacademic world of the student-athlete,
must be represented. Finally, there should be credible representation
from the ranks of the black student-athletes, black faculty, black student
leaders, and black administrators. Not only does such membership give
credence to the investigative body, it improves the likelihood of educating the entire community about the special needs of black student-
athletes on predominantly white campuses.

Now that we have the attention and respect of our constituencies
through careful selection of representatives, we need to define the problems clearly. Precise definition will inevitably give the problems of the
black student-athlete more credibility in the eyes of each constituency
and increase the likelihood of change.

...ave cast the problems of the black student-athlete in ...is important to sample scientifically the prevailing ...ions of those important constituencies within the ...niverse. Gauging faculty and student attitudes ...rcollegiate athletics in general and toward student-athletes ...particular provides important data. This data is a basis for conjecture of how constituencies perceive student-athletes, and allows us to draw certain conclusions about how they are treated. Most institutions also have the technology to access and analyze academic performance, distribution of academic major selections, academic progress, and retention of student-athletes and the student body as a whole. These studies are not costly, and they enable investigators to define the needs of the black student-athlete in objective terms. We believe that any investigation of this type at predominantly white institutions that enroll black student-athletes will reveal as needs those that we have identified in this chapter.

With areas of need identified, Lewin's (1948) model focuses next on change strategies. As we have suggested, there are creditable programs that have content validity relative to addressing individual needs of the student-athlete (for instance, programs in stress management, time management, and assertiveness training). But addressing the needs of the black student-athlete on the predominantly white campus means addressing a broader context of needs. We will review a few of these special needs and examine them through a systems approach.

Career Education Programs for Black Student-Athletes. Because of the emphasis placed on professional sports as a means of upward mobility, black student-athletes must be realistically and tactfully apprised of the odds against making a living in professional sports. We emphasize tact because, for many black athletes, athletic achievement is their only source of self-esteem. Not only should we help these students discover their career interests, values, and competencies, but we should introduce them to other successful career role models. Successful black business leaders and black faculty and administrators should be encouraged to share their experiences with these students. These experiences take on added importance for the black athlete (or any black student) at a predominantly white institution where successful black professionals are likely to be a barely visible minority.

Stress Management/Time Management Programs for Black Student-Athletes. The ubiquitous stress management program sometimes does injustice to the client in stress. We believe that when black student-athletes experience stress, it is an appropriate and normal reaction. Stress management strategies typically focus upon the individual as the target of change and encourage the individual to adapt to what we see as unreasonable circumstances. Since personal stress is often a reaction to overburdened time schedules, we find value in combining both stress management and time management into one program. Furthermore, such a combined program should be presented not only to the student-athlete, but to coaching staffs, athletic and academic administrators, and interested faculty. The goal here is twofold: first, to make those who control the athlete's life sensitive to the demands of being a good student and a good athlete; and second, to assist coaches and athletic administrators in dealing with the tremendous stress that they experience and to prevent that stress from being transferred to the athletes in their charge.

Resident Student Development Programs. It is typical of many big-time sports programs in the South and elsewhere to segregate athletes into exclusive housing complexes. The NCAA prohibits housing complexes composed exclusively of student-athletes, but athletic ghettos do exist on many campuses where a number of token nonathletes are permitted to live to satisfy the letter if not the spirit of this regulation. The argument for segregation is that athletes must have ready access to training facilities and coaches must have ready access to their athletes. Another purpose of exclusive housing is to control these students more effectively than would be possible if they were housed throughout the community.

A survey of 388 student-athletes at one institution discovered that fewer than one third preferred to live in housing composed exclusively of student athletes. Of those who actually lived in exclusive athletic housing complexes, more than half reported feeling "isolated from the rest of the student body." As a racial minority, black student-athletes feel sufficiently isolated on predominantly white campuses without adding the enforced isolation of exclusive housing. Members of the athletic and booster communities must be convinced that mainstreaming all student-athletes, the black student-athlete in particular, is in everyone's best interests. At the very least, if exclusive housing continues, student affairs administrators should insist on student affairs coordination as is the case in other student housing. Such an opportunity would allow student affairs administrators to have a direct impact on the lives of these student-athletes.

Peer Counseling/Personal Adjustment Programs. Black student-athletes who enroll at a predominantly white institution must have an opportunity to deal with personal and social issues that only they can truly understand. Peer-counseling programs offer the black student-athlete an outlet and facilitate adjustment. These programs should emanate from university counseling centers and should include non-athletes, both to sensitize the latter to the black student-athlete's unique circumstances and to allow student-athletes the opportunity to expand their reference group.

Study Skill/Academic Skill Development Programs. For academically underprepared black student-athletes, academic-skill and study-skill programs should not only teach skills but also seek to change attitudes of indifference toward academics. Students with inadequate academic skills should be encouraged to confront emotional resistance to academic tasks. A growing body of research is supporting the notion that cognitive skill development strategies alone are inadequate for students who perceive no reward for academic achievement (Noel and Levitz, 1982; Tobias, 1978). Combining these programs with peer counseling and personal adjustment programs would make such an effort more effective. In a broader sense, program administrators must also make faculty sensitive to the fact that the "dumb jock" may be a very discouraged learner whose potential remains to be discovered.

Revitalized Human Relations Programs. With the demise of the sixties and seventies and the passing of the heyday of the civil rights movement, race relations programs have become passé. Never before have they been so needed. It is true that blatant racism is less apparent than in the past; however, a more subtle and insidious institutional racism persists. One need only scan the ranks for black representation in any profession other than sports or entertainment to see that there is a strong basis for persistence of racism in our institutions. Black students on predominantly white campuses experience these feelings daily. Black student-athletes, as isolated as they are, tend to experience these pressures even more acutely. The roller coaster of experience that black student-athletes ride allows them to receive total community acceptance through exceptional athletic achievement, but they encounter indifference and even resentment in classes which are in most cases conducted by white instructors. The student affairs administrator must lead the way in devising training programs for coaching staff, faculty, students, and administrators to rouse us from our complacency about race issues and help us confront the many manifestations of institutional racism.

Outreach to Community/Booster Organizations. Many communities support the local institution's athletic programs with vigor, and, more important, dollars. Athletic booster organizations raise millions each year to help make their teams winners. Booster organizations in particular exert a powerful influence on the administration of many big-time athletic programs. Though well-meaning, these fans can cause harm to an institution's athletic program and to student-athletes. It is therefore critical that comprehensive programs to meet the needs of the black student-athlete include these outlying constituencies.

Unlike other students, there is a conflicting duality in the role of the student-athlete. Academicians on one side insist on the primacy of academic achievement. Avid fans on the other side insist on a winning team in return for their money. Faculty insist on regular class attendance while boosters clamor for more college baseball games that would make regular class attendance impossible. Ignorant of the demands of the others, constituencies exert pressure on the student-athlete that often creates conflicts too overwhelming for the individual to resolve.

It is important that there be a balance to the academic and athletic sides of the student-athlete equation. Student affairs administrators should seek to influence booster decision-making and to make these organizations sensitive to the pressures imposed on student-athletes. We can no longer ignore the influence that this important constituency has on the lives of black and white student-athletes. Institutionalizing a program that involves a number of constituencies requires a demonstration of the program's value to each constituency. Consequently, each program must have an evaluation component which demonstrates both the internal consistency of the intervention and the external value to the interested constituencies. In the unfreezing stage, we discussed academic performance measures as one way to objectively gauge progress in meeting the needs of black student-athletes. These same measures can be employed to periodically judge the effectiveness of our comprehensive program of interventions. Quality-of-life issues, however, are far more difficult to measure. We cannot surmise an improvement in one's life prospects from an improvement in grades. It is more important that student affairs administrators regularly communicate with black student athletes. Ultimately, we must use our intuitive sense to gauge progress in this area.

Developing program interventions on behalf of black student-athletes does not create change. It creates a mechanism for change. Refreezing should not occur until minimum goals have been reached. The juggernaut of big-time college sports may have to be slowed considerably before this can happen. A day of reckoning may be near. Proceeding on its current course, the business of big-time intercollegiate sports may collapse under its own weight, or it may be forced to unmask its facade of amateurism and openly join the ranks of professionalism that it is rapidly approaching. Meanwhile, there is a constituency in need on our campuses — black student-athletes. While we have addressed our attention mostly to black male athletes concentrated in the revenue-earning sports, the spectre of exploitation is also haunting the female ranks, and the measures we have described will be more appropriate for them as the duality of their roles becomes more pronounced.

We have described methods of influencing institutional policy on behalf of black athletes that are simple to understand. We do not mean to imply by any means that they are easy to implement. The student affairs administrator must take a moral reading of his or her own feelings about this issue and make a personal decision about the level of commitment he or she is willing to make. We are convinced that any detailed examination of the plight of black student-athletes on predominantly white college campuses will elevate the sense of urgency about their situation. We are also convinced that the student affairs administrator must be prepared to move beyond individual interventions to confront a system of abuse if lasting progress on behalf of black athletes is to be made.

References

Bandura, A. (Ed.). *Psychological Modeling: Conflicting Theories.* Atherton, 1971a.

Bandura, A. "Psychotherapy Based upon Modeling Principles." In A. Bergin and S. Garfield (Eds.), *Handbook of Psychotherapy and Behavior Change.* New York: Wiley, 1971b.

Edwards, H. "Educating Black Athletes." *The Atlantic Monthly,* 1983, *252* (2), 31–38.

Edwards, H. "The Black Athlete in America: Taking Responsibility." Presented as part of the lecture series "Sports in America" at Florida State University, March 28, 1984.

Gross, E. "Universities as Organizations: A Research Approach." In Y. Hasenfeld and R. English (Eds.), *Human Services Organizations.* Ann Arbor: University of Michigan Press, 1977.

Haughey, E. "Intrusive Advising." In L. Noel and R. Levitz (Eds.), *How to Succeed with Academically Underprepared Students: A Catalog of Successful Practices.* Iowa City: American College Testing Program, 1982.

Kozol, J. *Death at an Early Age.* Boston: Houghton Mifflin, 1967.

Lewin, K. *Resolving Social Conflicts.* New York: Harper, 1948.

Noel, L., and Levitz, R. (Eds.). *How to Succeed with Academically Underprepared Students: A Catalog of Successful Practices.* Iowa City: American College Testing Program, 1982.

President's Committee on the Student Athlete. Unpublished survey of student-athletes at Florida State University, Tallahassee, January 1984a.

President's Committee on the Student Athlete. Unpublished survey of faculty at Florida State University, Tallahassee, February 1984b.

President's Committee on the Student Athlete. *Student Athletes at the Florida State University: Planning Responsibility.* Report presented by the President's Committee on the Student Athlete, Florida State University, Tallahassee, April 17, 1984c.

Rosenthal, R. *Pygmalion in the Classroom.* New York: Holt, Rinehart & Winston, 1968.

Smith, L. N., Lippitt, R., Noel, L., and Sprandel, D. *Mobilizing the Campus for Retention: An Innovative Quality of Life Model.* Iowa City: American College Testing Program, 1981.

"Sport Editorial." *Florida Times Union,* June 4, 1980.

Tobias, S. *Overcoming Math Anxiety.* New York: Norton, 1978.

Underwood, J. "Student Athletes: The Sham, the Shame." *Sports Illustrated,* May 19, 1980, 36–45.

Warfield, J. "Letters." *The Chronicle of Higher Education,* 1984, *28* (11), 35.

Wittmer, J., Bostic, D., Phillips, T. D., and Waters, W. "The Personal, Academic, and Career Problems of College Student Athletes: Some Possible Answers." *The Personnel and Guidance Journal,* 1981, *60* (1), 52–55.

Wolfe, H., and others (Eds.). *Webster's New Collegiate Dictionary.* Springfield, Mass.: Merriam, 1981.

Audiovisual Sources

Columbia Broadcasting System. "Losers." *60 Minutes,* February 3, 1980.

Public Broadcasting Service. "Chasing the Basketball Dream." *Blacks in Sport,* April 29, 1984.

Bob Leach is vice-president for student affairs at Florida State University in Tallahassee, and president-elect of the National Association of Student Personnel Administrators (NASPA). An avid amateur athlete and father of a college athlete, he is committed to providing athletic opportunities for all students. He recently chaired a university committee investigating widely publicized allegations brought by a basketball player against Florida State University and its athletic department.

Bob Conners is a research associate with the Division of Student Affairs at Florida State University. For the past four years he has counseled, advised, and taught student-athletes, and recently served on the President's Committee on the Student Athlete at Florida State University.

The backgrounds of many student-athletes and the unique
demands placed upon them in college indicate a need for
programs designed to enhance their educational and
personal development.

Providing Academic and Psychological Services for the College Athlete

Robert B. Hurley
Robin L. Cunningham

Anyone interested enough to have picked up this sourcebook and persistent enough to have read this far is undoubtedly aware of the controversy surrounding major college athletics. It is rare that a week goes by without seeing an article in the press exposing some scandal involving college athletic programs. Underwood (1980) and Michener (1976) have written eloquently on the topic. Colleges and universities have been accused of sacrificing their academic integrity in order to develop competitive athletic teams that will appear on television and draw huge crowds, producing increased revenues at a time when the traditional college-age population is shrinking. They have also been accused of compromising their moral integrity by cynically using gifted athletes for four years of athletic eligibility. The athletes then either do not graduate, or they are granted degrees even though they are appallingly illiterate and poorly equipped to handle a life without the glamour associated with athletic renown.

A. Shriberg, F. R. Brodzinski (Eds.). *Rethinking Services for College Athletes.* New Directions for Student Services, no. 28. San Francisco: Jossey-Bass, December 1984.

There have been several responses to these charges both from the athletic establishment and from universities themselves. The National Collegiate Athletic Association (NCAA), comprised of both top school and athletic administrators, has moved to tighten admissions standards for student-athletes (the controversial Proposition 48) and normal progress rules governing academic eligibility to participate in intercollegiate athletics.

In addition, the National Association of Academic Athletic Advisors (NAAAA) was founded in 1976. Its membership grows almost geometrically as more institutions become aware of the special needs of student-athletes, especially those on scholarship in the high-revenue producing sports of basketball and football. More full- and part-time positions, bearing a variety of job titles, are being created for those who are charged with maintaining the institution's academic and moral integrity. These advisers are generally involved in varying degrees in most of the following activities: providing information for recruiting, orientation, monitoring programs, liaison with the faculty and other university services, tutoring, remediation, course advising, counseling, and placement upon graduation. NCAA regulations stipulate that student-athletes on scholarship shall not receive any services that are not available to the student body as a whole. All of the above services are available to the entire student body, but their utilization is voluntary and nonsystematic. Academic advisement programs are different in that the student-athletes are systematically exposed to these services through explicit cooperation between the athletic department and the adviser or advisers.

Ideally, the coaching staff subscribes to the priority implicit in the phrase *student-athlete*. In the real world, however, the relationship between academic advisers and coaches is not always smooth. Some coaches, pressured to produce wins and hence revenue, often give lip service to the student-athlete concept but actually behave in a different way. Some are quite candid about it. Michener (1976) describes what the late Paul (Bear) Bryant, former University of Alabama football coach, said of the concept:

> I used to go along with the idea that football players on scholarship were 'student-athletes', which is what the NCAA calls them. Meaning a student first, an athlete second. We were kidding ourselves, trying to make it more palatable to the academicians. We don't have to say that and we shouldn't. At the level we play, the boy is an athlete first and a student second" [p. 203].

This view is not unique to Bear Bryant and the University of Alabama. Coaches who share this view will recruit students on the basis of their athletic ability alone, will pressure admissions officials to admit some athletes who may be high-risk students, and will see the academic adviser as one whose job is to keep the athlete eligible, even if that means the athlete is to major in eligibility. Operationally, *majoring in eligibility* means taking "gut" courses only—whether they will constitute a major needed for graduation or not—and avoiding difficult courses that may mean either low grades that threaten eligibility or time-consuming study that may take away from the student-athlete's primary athletic commitment. Some coaches may also see the academic adviser as one who takes care of everything for the student-athlete, leaving the athlete free to devote himself more fully to the athletic task at hand, unencumbered by bureaucratic matters inherent in college life. The athletes themselves, being human, may all too easily succumb to this paternalism. Hence, the academic adviser may find that he or she is caught in the middle between the conflicting role expectations of the athletic department, the student, and faculty.

Unique Demands on Student-Athletes

The needs of student-athletes are special because of the unique demands that are placed upon their time, energies, and egos as a consequence of their athletic participation. Erik Erikson (Erikson and Funkenstein, 1959, p. 74) has observed that the university is "society's most elaborate device for the artificial postponement of adulthood that could be imagined." This statement may be even more accurate for the student-athlete than for the nonathlete. If the achievement of an adult identity is, as Marcia (1980) says, a result of experiencing a developmental "crisis" and making a commitment to others, to an occupation, and to an ideology, then participation in big-time intercollegiate athletics can forestall rather than facilitate one's optimal development. If the life of the typical college student is not real, then what is the life of the typical big-time college athlete?

Time and Energy. The football season begins in early August and lasts, for most, through mid-December—four months. Athletes on scholarship must perform weight training during the off-season until spring practice begins. When that is over, the conditioning expectation is there again. A football player can never forget that he is there to play football.

Basketball is no different. Unofficial conditioning programs begin immediately in the fall. Official practice begins on October 15, and the season runs until mid-March. Seven of the nine months in the school year are devoted to basketball. Practices in both sports are usually three hours long. In both, game films need to be screened and strategy discussed. Perhaps time needs to be spent on the training table or in a whirlpool bath. Weekends are taken up and classes missed because of travel time to and from games. Work-study students are permitted to work a maximum of twenty hours per week, but student-athletes devote more time than that during the season to their sport. Vacations for other students may mean just more of the same for student-athletes.

Practices are physically draining. Coaches seek perfect execution, and for this, drill and repetition are necessary. What always came easy and was usually fun becomes, for many, drudgery. All college students need to learn to manage their time and energy to adjust to the new life-style and hours. For the student-athlete, it is most important. When students miss classes due to athletic schedules, they may also miss quizzes, announcements of quizzes, mid-terms, long-range assignments, and so on. They especially need help in learning how to keep in contact with their professors and their nonathlete classmates.

Psychological Demands. In a way, the student-athlete on scholarship in a big-time college athletic program has a reasonable expectation of achieving his career goal—professional athletics. He probably has heard many times that only 2 percent of those who participate in intercollegiate athletics ever sign a professional contract (Berkow, 1983). But he has relatively good reason to believe that he will be one of that 2 percent. He has been acclaimed for his athletic prowess since he was in junior high school. He has been on all-star teams. Adults and peers have lavished status and prestige on him. He has been recruited by a college that all sports fans have heard of. Maybe teachers, coaches, and counselors made things easy for him, knowing he would go to college because of his athletic ability. He sees himself as a physical rather than as an intellectual person. Because of the success he achieved as an athlete, his senior year in high school was a delight, and most of the joy came from his excellence in sports.

But now he is a freshman in college. Athletically, he is surrounded by others who were all-stars—just as strong, quick, fast, tall, and so on. In high school, plays had been run over and over for him. Here he must pay his dues, fit into this team of stars, and adjust to a secondary role. His weaknesses become apparent, and coaches get on his back, trying to get him to improve. His playing time is limited or nonexistent. His dreams of a professional career are shaken, maybe even shattered. Academically, he must make the same adjustments that other freshmen must make. He may be more ill-equipped than they to make it because he has neglected his academic skills in high school, because of the athletic demands made on his time and energies, and because he has only viewed a college as a means of achieving his athletic goals. But if his athletic dreams are shaken, and he is not able by aptitude or interest to get by academically, what will become of him?

Socially he may, like so many college freshmen, be among strangers. He may be in a racial or socioeconomic environment different from his own. His athletic participation sets him apart—hero to some, stereotyped and dismissed by some, unknown to others. These reactions of the student body, and the usual encouragement of his coaches, forces him to isolate himself, to find his "family" with his teammates and the coaching staff. He may be homesick like so many others. He may miss his girlfriend. He may wonder why he ever came to this strange place.

Although we have discussed these academic, athletic, psychological, and social factors separately, they are of course interrelated. Loneliness affects academic and athletic performance, poor athletic performance affects academic performance, and so on. How can one with so much promise return home a failure? Many nonathletic college students face the same problems. The difference with the athlete is, however, that the institution encourages the dream, recruits him or her to its athletic program, and creates the demands on his or her time and energy. The reward for the expenditure of his energy is room, board, tuition, and books—a college education. The reward may be something he does not want, or does not think he needs. If that is the reward we offer, and if we seem to be placing obstacles in the way of achieving it, we are bound by our consciences to provide all the help we can in overcoming these obstacles, and it needs to be both academic and psychological in nature.

Academic Support. Academic support services should begin when the athlete is first brought on campus for a recruiting visit. Many coaches, well-intentioned though they may be, are not familiar with the requirements of all programs in a large university. An interview with an academic adviser should be included in this visit. Hopefully, the recruit will have provided some information regarding his high school academic record—courses taken, grades, results of standardized tests, and so on. If it appears that remedial programs are necessary, these programs should be explained. If the student-athlete has expressed a choice of major, the requirements of that major should be explained. The academic service program should be described at this time, and academic eligibility requirements should be delineated. The basic message to be conveyed is, "We want you to graduate. We will do all that we can to help you do that, but ultimately whether you graduate or not is up to you. If the student suffers from a learning disability, and there is no established program on the campus designed to help students with that disability, the student should not be admitted.

Orientation. Once admitted, the student should be encouraged to attend the regular orientation session to facilitate his integration into college life. At this time, testing that is needed should be done, and placement decisions should be made on the basis of these results, his high school record, and his goals. The first-semester schedule should, of course, be planned at this time, keeping in mind the practice and game schedules in order to avoid conflicts between athletic and academic commitments.

Communication with Faculty. The academic adviser should initiate contact with all student-athletes' course instructors, especially for new students. Information regarding attendance, grades, completion of assignments, participation, and need for tutoring should be sought. Of course, not all faculty will cooperate in this venture, thinking that college students should not be coddled. Although there is merit in this view, efforts should be made to establish open communication to prevent academic difficulties before they occur. The basic goal is to maintain academic and moral integrity and competitive athletic programs. Achieving that goal is a boon to the entire community.

Study Halls. All entering student athletes should be required to attend a study hall at a regularly scheduled time. Traditionally, this study hall has been held in the evenings, but Nixon (1983) has argued convincingly for a daytime study hall integrated into class schedules to enable tired athletes to have evenings free. Once a student has demonstrated that he can combine athletic involvement and academic success in the interest of developing a sense of independence, study hall may be made optional.

Tutoring. Tutoring should not be confused with or substituted for studying. As used here, tutoring refers to extra teaching to help a student better understand what he does not comprehend after studying. Students who experience difficulties should be encouraged first to contact the course instructor, who may recommend tutoring and tutors. The academic adviser should coordinate this service, monitoring the performance of both students and tutors.

Advisement and Registration. The academic adviser should maintain records on the academic progress of all student-athletes. The goal is to help students choose a major and to select a major adviser as soon as possible. The academic adviser should then maintain contact with each departmental adviser. It is our position that student-athletes, who devote so much time to representing the institution, should be given preference in registration so that they may schedule courses that minimize the conflict between athletic and academic commitments.

Research. The academic adviser should also keep records that enable him or her to provide graduation rate data for scholarship and nonscholarship student-athletes in all sports. These records should also be used to determine academic eligibility as it is defined by the NCAA, by the institution, and by the athletic conference of which it is a member. It is suggested also that athletic honor rolls be published by team within the institution to dispel the "dumb jock" image and capitalize on competitive instincts of student-athletes.

Liaison with University Services. Academic advisers should serve as referral agents for all campus services (housing, financial aid, bursar, registrar, remedial services, and so on). Contacts must not be made for the athletes. It is important for them, if they are to develop as fully functioning adults, to learn how to deal with others and how to make their wants known in an assertive manner to develop a sense of competence in managing their own affairs. The adviser's role is to point them in the right direction, to help them develop the interpersonal skills needed to act in their own best interests, and to allow them to try their skills.

Placement. Academic advisers should at least oversee job placement of graduating athletes. Ideally, the student-athlete, at the end of the program, should be mainstreamed, and should be encouraged to use the institution's regular placement services. He should be encouraged to develop and follow-up on job leads, and should be taught the usual resumé preparation and interviewing skills.

Psychological Services. Student-athletes need someone with whom they can share their dreams, fears, disappointments, and questions. Regular individual counseling appointments should be established on at least a bi-weekly basis. It is most important in this counseling relationship to establish its confidential nature. Many times, athletes must keep up a facade with their teammates, and fear reprisals in loss of playing time from their coaches if they are honest and express negative thoughts. *Group counseling* can also be very helpful to student-athletes, and may even develop greater cohesion in team sports with fewer players. Again, confidentiality is important. If athletes, socialized to act a particular way, can learn to take risks and be open with others, their personal development can be greatly enhanced. Another form of assistance is *group guidance,* a more leader-centered, educationally focused group that meets with a specific goal. This is a useful way to teach assertiveness training, decision making, time management, study skills, and so on. All these skills are extremely helpful to the development of student-athletes.

Organizational Considerations

The program described above should be funded by and should report to the vice-president for academic affairs, and should service all student-athletes. At least one member of the advisement team should be a faculty member. Service offices should not be located in an athletic department facility. This view is apparently at variance with what exists. Brennan (1983) surveyed 84 NAAAA members, and reports that the typical academic adviser is a male under 35 years old who has been employed less than three years. His salary is in the $20,000-$25,000 range, and he is paid by the athletic department, reports to the athletic director, and works out of an athletic administration facility. He holds a master's degree in education and has coaching experience. Thirty-nine percent of these advisers are the first to hold the position.

It is most important, in terms of both form and substance, that the service be associated with the academic area of the institution in order to communicate to the entire community that the emphasis of the program is on the *student*-athlete. The cooperation of the athletic department and the coaching staffs is important in terms of recruiting and in terms of disciplining the recalcitrant student. That is where their commitment to academic integrity can be made manifest.

References

Berkow, I. "College Factories and Their Output." *New York Times,* January 18, 1983, p. 25.

Brennan, T. "Academic Athletic Advising; A Job Description Statement." Unpublished manuscript, University of New Mexico, 1983.

Erikson, E. H., and Funkenstein, D. J. (Eds.). *The Student and Mental Health: An International View.* New York: World Federation for Mental Health, 1959.

Marcia, J. E. "Identity in Adolescence." In J. Adelson (Ed.), *Handbook of Adolescent Psychology.* New York: Wiley, 1980.

Michener, J. A. *Sports in America.* New York: Random House, 1976.

Nixon, A. "Molding Minds When the Sun Shines, Or an Experiment with Daytime Study Hall." Unpublished manuscript, University of Nevada, Las Vegas, 1983.

Underwood, J. "The Writing Is on the Wall." *Sports Illustrated,* May 19, 1980, pp. 38–72.

Robert B. Hurley is faculty representative to athletics at Seton Hall University, South Orange, New Jersey.

Robin L. Cunningham is a graduate assistant in the athletic department at Seton Hall University. A former collegiate athlete, she serves as academic adviser to athletes.

*How does the chilef student affairs officer manage the
expanding, demanding, and challenging campus athletic
department? New roles and the responsibilities for the CSAO,
once learned, can produce a healthy interaction which supports
athletes, the department, the division, and the institution.*

Supervising College Athletics—
The Role of the Chief Student
Affairs Officer

Dennis C. Golden

Intercollegiate athletics have become a major force on America's campuses. Colleges and universities devote more personnel and money to athletics than many realize. Athletics consume large portions of administrative time and resources, and their effects on our campuses are often honorable and delightful. All too frequently, however, as Michener (1976) points out, athletics have been accused of generating some of the most difficult, deplorable, and embarrassing institutional problems. Moreover, Michener (1976) states that a critical analysis of intercollegiate athletics has been grossly neglected. In far too many instances, universities take major positions on numerous issues affecting their institutions, but consistently avoid an analysis of athletics and their role in the university environment.

The era of blind acceptance of athletics is past. Its demise was spurred by the prospects of declining student enrollments and the ensuing financial crunch, compounded by the inability of many institutions to finance capital improvements, adequate staff, faculty compensation, and purchases of new academic equipment. The entire world of inter-

A. Shriberg, F. R. Brodzinski (Eds.). *Rethinking Services for College Athletes.* New Directions
for Student Services, no. 28. San Francisco: Jossey-Bass, December 1984.

collegiate athletics — personnel, budgets, philosophy, booster clubs, media relations, and ethics — needs to be subjected to careful study and scrutiny. Those who promote athletics and their enormous budgets will have to justify those programs more than ever before. Many preconceptions will be challenged. In the forefront of such a study should be the chief student affairs officer (CSAO). This chapter will examine the critical role of the CSAO in such areas as relations with coaches and players, academic support, psychological needs of athletes, housing, athlete identity, discipline, and recruiting.

The Nature of Athletics

In addition to academic certification, campuses need to produce people with emotion, heart, dedication, a sense of shared mission, and proven competencies. In this sense, athletics may be viewed as a miniature model of life. From participant to spectator, it is acknowledged that form, function, and focus in athletics is reasonably clear. Athletic competition is judged not with reference to outside and accidental attributes, but by the combination of physical vigor and moral qualities which comprise athletic prowess.

Essentially, in its most desired form, athletics displays not the works of machines but the wonders of young people exhibiting teamwork, ingenuity, hard work, and fortitude. To participate in athletics is to become a member of a unique minority group. This minority group is based not on social status, financial resources, or skin color but on a social adhesive that binds through a burning desire to win, dedication to a shared mission, recognition that individual success is secondary to group success, and a commitment to abide by the rules of fair play.

This is also a minority group that is judged by what they do and not by what they say, and the results are part of the public record for all to see. The ultimate competitive creed for a member of this minority group is to realize that the greatest moments of competitive happiness are found when the athlete is tested beyond the breaking point and then does not break or fail. This is weighty material for young adults; yet we expect our athletes to handle it in a mature manner.

The CSAO and Athletics

Sports and other forms of vigorous physical activity provide educational experiences which cannot be duplicated in the classroom. They are an uncompromising laboratory in which we must think and act quickly and efficiently under pressure, and they force us to meet our own inadequacies face to face . . . as nothing else does.
      U.S. Supreme Court Justice Byron R. White
      All-American football player, University of Colorado

In many institutions, especially in the big-time intercollegiate sports programs, the athletic department does not report to the CSAO. A major premise of this chapter is that in institutions of higher learning, the department should do so. A key concern of the CSAO is therefore how best to administer all campus-based athletics, especially football and basketball programs that have assumed a semi-professional nature at numerous institutions and a blatantly professional stature at others (Michener, 1976).

The role and responsibility of the CSAO in athletics evolves from the reality that the primary reason for a college or university's existence is intellectual. As Blake (1979, p. 281) states, "The formal curriculum is ultimately the reason that the students attend an institution. However, what occurs outside the classroom is an equally vital and compelling part of the students' total educational immersion."

This is especially true for student-athletes because for them campus life differs from ordinary life by virtue of its direction, demands, and scope of commitment. Student-athletes are placed in a highly intensive and challenging environment. They strive to become masters of their own destiny, which for them means to win. But the question arises as to what is happening to them developmentally as they endeavor to win. Additionally, many persons equate success in athletics with the belief that the institution is performing its administrative functions respectably. But is it true that if colleges or universities are having success in athletics, then they are performing their administrative functions respectably?

For the CSAO, it is most important to have a philosophy of sport that is congruent with the institution's mission, goals, and objectives. This is a philosophy that predicates the reality of the often stated yet seldom actualized term *student-athlete*. Organizationally, athletic programs and athletic directors should report to the CSAO, who in turn reports to the chief executive officer (CEO). This is important because athletics are developmental in nature, and they need the attention of a CSAO who embodies the college or university to athletic administrators, coaches, support staff, and athletes. The CSAO should also interpret and, when necessary, enforce rules and regulations that affect athletes individually and collectively. This is a very important concept. According to Blake (1979), the CSAO should be able to encompass the institution in its entirety—including its physical arrangements, its human dimensions, its legal realities, and its effect on multiple publics. The CSAO's relationship with the athletic department is demanding and diverse, and certain beliefs must be stated that are helpful for those involved on a lifelong rather than a short-term basis.

Critical Aspects of Athletic Administration

The Two Giants. The CSAO should focus on football and basketball, since these sports present the most pressing moral and financial concerns. As Michener (1976) points out, in time of financial stringency one cannot escape from making certain value judgments relating to these two sports. For the most part, other athletic programs are not beset by problems associated with recruiting and expenditure of large sums of money that leads to outrageous commercialism that has the tail wagging the dog at too many institutions.

The CSAO — Ready for the Challenge? Many CSAOs feel insecure and inadequate in athletic circles. They generally were not intercollegiate athletes, and they feel that most athletic programs seem to operate without them or in spite of them. However, the CSAO should be the administrative link between the institution's CEO and the athletic department. Furthermore, the CSAO should help the CEO to become visibly and directly involved with the athletic teams through planned press conferences or meetings that include locker room visits. Additionally, the CSAO should reaffirm the institution's mission, goals, objectives, and academic requirements to both coaches and players in a timely and effective manner.

Coaches Need Support. Too many football and basketball coaches live in the fast lane. They have high salaries, cars, expense accounts, endorsements, and so on, yet they are frequently found to be insecure because they are not sure they are accepted or appreciated even when they are winning. Their world of tactics, travel, tickets, recruiting, and media relations is very stressful. All too often these coaches become virtual strangers in their own homes. They may beome alienated from their spouses and children, and they need the CSAO's understanding and support. This task is made easier if the athletic department is part of the CSAO's organization. In addition, the CSAO should provide the athletic director and coaches with decent long-term contracts. If he or she wants to leave before the contract expires, hold them to it or seriously consider having the new employer buy out the contract. This will safeguard your institution's investment in your athletic staff.

Do's and Don't's of Hiring a Coach. This is an experience unlike any other in higher education, including selecting a president. Affirmative action and equal opportunity procedures are seldom, if ever, followed. Little time is spent investigating the prospective coach's educational background and value system. Seldom is an on-site follow-up conducted on the coach's current campus by speaking to administrators, staff, and players. No one wants to find a flaw in the ideal candidate.

How often have we heard the cry to hire a qualified name coach? Qualified for what? Name prominence based on what criteria? How many times do we have to relearn the lesson that the win-loss record isn't enough?

The CSAO has an obligation to ascertain the coach's graduation ratio, recruiting and working philosophies, public statements, and career goals. Many CSAOs are not familiar with the details of coaching contracts that may include elaborate fringe benefits such as expense accounts, credit cards, country club memberships, and cars. But these deals do exist nationwide, and it is better to be knowledgeable about them rather than helplessly reactive when the president asks for your assistance.

Equity. The institution must provide sufficient support to the athletic department so that there is a clear and reasonable chance for success. This means providing sufficient resources to win and to produce good athletes, graduates, and citizens. Colleges and universities cannot tolerate cheating in recruiting or grades, yet one must realize that strong social mores are alive and well on our campuses. Hypocrisy abounds, and athletes will not "squeal" because they are fearful they will be ostracized from their group. The CSAO must therefore serve as a watchdog for the athletic director, coaches, and players. Cheating should be immediate grounds for discussion, investigation, decision, and possible dismissal.

Remember that coaches come and go, and that no coach has the right to play with the collective reputation of an entire institution. Colleges and universities continually learn that, in the eyes of the National Collegiate Athletic Association (NCAA) and the media, ignorance or benign neglect are insufficient or blatant violations.

Dealing with the Jealousy Factor. The CSAO should help coaches and players understand that they are subject to frequent subliminal jealousy. In some ways, this is because they are a bright, young, virile, healthy, and strong group. It is also because they are truly performance-based, and when the contest is over, the spoils go to the victor. Other constituencies within academe are envious of such a closure on any project.

Player-Coach Relationships. The player-coach relationship can be considered a cliché these days. A CSAO must learn early that coaches and athletes need one another and are reluctant to inform on each other. For informational purposes, the CSAO needs to establish and maintain a communications network that involves trainers, ticket takers, the sports information director, bus drivers, the food service, and housing staff.

The CSAO must also realize that many athletes have cyclical developmental crises—for instance, the starter-to-substitute and the substitute-to-starter syndromes. Similarly, many athletes are frequently vulnerable people and have a desire to understand their relationship to God. A chaplain's affiliation with athletic programs is therefore as important, and sometimes more important, than the player-coach relationship.

The Athletic Identity. The CSAO must understand that student-athletes are subject to massive identity confusion. They frequently wonder if they belong to the general student body, or only to the subculture of the team. They are aware of their size, bulk, height, and muscle. All these attributes have their place in athletics, but how do those who possess them really feel about themselves as individuals and not as athletic entertainers? Competitors all possess the fear of failure and the exhilaration associated with success. They are anxious about their performance levels and they need honest responses.

Psychological Needs Are Important. The CSAO should not wait until the athlete needs assistance because of probable and predictable problems with sex, drugs, thefts, gambling, assaults, and other matters. Nondirect therapy does not usually work well with student-athletes. Direct intervention counseling methods are needed. Because of the intensive preparatory and performance aspects of intercollegiate athletics, student-athletes are pushed much closer to the edge than non-athletes. Therefore, support systems must be planned and placed in an operational mode very early in the athlete's collegiate career.

The Recruiting World. The CSAO should know how much money is spent by whom and for whom. Additionally, the CSAO should help the athletic director and coaches understand the person who should be brought to the institution as a student-athlete. This stems from the CSAO's knowledge of the immediate and long-term institutional fit. Administrative direction and supervision is important when one considers that coaches can distribute thousands of dollars in scholarship money.

Social Shyness. Numerous athletes are shy and lacking in social skills. Many have not had the time or the opportunities to enhance their interpersonal skills because of the hours, days, weeks, and months spent preparing for their competitive experiences. The CSAO should work in a developmental framework to guide and assist them.

The Color Line. Performance, not talk, counts in athletics. When blacks and whites are mutually motivated toward the accomplishment of shared goals, when gestures such as hugs and high fives are made, it is a lesson that has far-reaching effects. There is no longer a color line in sports. The CSAO should take advantage of this reality and broaden the base of social equity, justice, and harmony throughout the campus.

Disciplining. Countless are the times when student life administrators are charged with the responsibility of disciplining athletes. Discipline should be sure and swift, since the athletic director and coaches should have a very clear understanding of the campus rules and regulations. One must realize, however, that to discipline an athlete in a manner that is the same for all other students is not always proper or appropriate.

To prevent a varsity athlete from participating in sports is necessary at times, but always remember that such sanctions are more severe than preventing other students from playing intramurals or participating in cocurricular activities. The athlete frequently hurts more, learns faster, and needs less sanction time than one might expect. A key is to remember that campus judicial systems should have an educational purpose and should be geared toward behavioral modification. Such a focus helps avoid the extremes of punitive excess or extreme leniency. Of course, there are times when separation from the team, school, or both is needed, and the CSAO must be prepared to initiate, support, and enforce such decisions no matter what the outcry from coaches, players, parents, media, alumni, and the general public.

Academic Support. Many coaches, unless told otherwise, will tell you that their job is to win contests. Because of this objective, and because coaches were generally not honor students during their college careers, one cannot expect coaches to remedy the sorry fact that many athletes are not prepared for the academic curriculum. All concerned must be helped by tutoring programs and academic supervisors for their student-athletes. This support staff should report to the academic vice-president, should be on a full-time basis, and should have the authority to confer with a player if he or she does not measure up to the required academic standards. The CSAO's responsibility is to be a catalyst for this operation, since the absence of such a system may have dire consequences for the athletic program and the institution's reputation.

Housing. Special housing for athletes does not serve a purpose beyond that of control and confinement. It is a life-limiting experience to be surrounded by actual and proclaimed "super jocks" for twenty-four hours a day. Conversation is often salty and shallow, and psychosocial development is frequently limited to other team members who have neither the desire nor the capacity to discuss anything except sports. Special housing also pampers the athlete in a manner that is neither mature nor meaningful in light of the pressures to be faced in later years.

Food. Training tables for football, basketball, and certain other sports are absolutely necessary, because the nutritional needs of the athlete far surpass those of the noncompetitor. The CSAO should actively support this need.

Working with the NCAA. This powerful body sets standards for conduct and operation in intercollegiate athletics. Very few CSAOs (approximately two dozen) were at the past two NCAA conventions. Operational, financial, academic, and governance matters should be the shared domain of the CSAO and the athletic director. At the convention, the NCAA conducts a two-day marathon business meeting of the highest order. If the CSAO has informational shortfall about such matters, it is a classic error in administrative judgment.

The Sports Information Director (SID). Since the role of the SID involves presenting clear, concise, and accurate information about athletic programs, it is much more effective to have the SID organizationally accountable to the athletic director within the student life division.

Perspective on Fans. Spectator judgments are fast and furious. Fans attend games by virtue of a free choice, using their own time and money. They cannot understand why teams should be "flat" or have an "off day." Because of a set number of regular-season contests, fans expect flawless performance at all times. Many coaches and players never really consider this fact and the deep-seated fan fury that can result if the outcome is anything less than a victory. Many a fan has been known to say, "We love you, win or tie—just don't tie too many." The CSAO should speak to the coaches and players about this factor and prepare them for dealing with fan pressures.

Minimum Evaluation. Earlier in this chapter it was indicated that coaches are frequently evaluated on the basis of their win-loss record. Too often we rationalize that as long as the coach is winning, the essence of the program is good. This is not always the case. The athletic director and the coaches should be formally and periodically evaluated, using the same or similar criteria used for other members of the student life division. Be assertive and fair with members of the athletic department. They will respect themselves and you in the process.

Maximum Evaluation. Such an evaluation is a human judgmental process that is used to provide information for decisions about people and programs. Athletics are people-oriented, performance-based activities. Therefore, evaluation is absolutely necessary to assure the proper roles, relationships, and responsibilities for players and coaches within the academic environment.

Within such a system, the CSAO has the opportunity to remind the athletic director and coaches that they evaluate players constantly. Checks are made on their height, weight, speed, techniques, quality point average (Q.P.A.), and so on, but seldom are checks make on their heads and hearts. Coaches also are evaluated constantly, whether they like it or not, by the media, alumni, the student newspaper, and fans. Yet the most important evaluation — what the players think — is all too often ignored. Therefore, Golden (1980) recommends the implementation of a three-part annual evaluation system that includes: (1) player self-evaluation, (2) player team evaluation, and (3) player evaluation of coaches. The third phase is the key to the process, and schools may benefit from having Declarations of Coaching that members of the athletic department sign and that are then used as a basis for annual evaluation.

The Budget. Many CSAOs have learned that the athletic budget is one of the most carefully guarded secrets in higher education. To obtain an accurate analysis of revenues and expenses requires skill, diplomacy, and a trust level of the highest professional order. Institutions are frequently embarrassed that their athletic budgets are in the red. Yet budget committees and boards of trustees permit this because they have determined that it is in the best interests of the institution to do so. This is a very difficult dilemma for CSAOs, who need more money for residence life, retention, counseling, health services, commuters, and other student services. In such situations, the CSAO is well-advised to understand the power bases, and then to take steps to remedy the fiscal problem on a sound and programmatic basis.

Other Students and Those in Non-Revenue Sports. The general student body and those participating in lifetime, recreational, and intramural sports should be better understood and respected by the varsity athletes. Essentially, all other students are stockholders in the varsity programs, and the varsity athletes should relate to them in a mature and meaningful manner.

Booster Clubs. Because of financial constraints, booster clubs are necessary in order to raise funds on many campuses. When such clubs are planned or in operation, the CSAO should see that the club director is an institutional employee and that this person reports directly to an institutional executive who is responsible for business and management or university relations and development. This will enable the club to realize its objective in a safe and solvent manner. It will also avoid the classic conflict of interests that result if the club operates within the athletic department per se.

Is There Life After Sports? When eligibility expires or an injury cuts short an athlete's career, there is still a lifetime to face. There are tragic situations in which athletes criticize both their sport and their institution in later years because they feel the school used them and never prepared them for postcollege life. When former players and coaches choose not to associate with each other, something is drastically wrong with the athletic experience. For a coach not to be able to look a former player in the eye is an all-too-frequent, damaging, and devastating reality.

The CSAO must educate the athletic staff to look beyond the immediacy of the win-loss syndrome, and should strive to give coaches and players a lifelong perspective and appreciation of their competitive experiences. If this is done, fewer student-athletes will feel that they have been used and dealt with in a pragmatic and unethical manner.

Conclusion

The CSAO and others must realize that revenue-producing sports that student-athletes participate in are not likely to be lifetime pursuits. Thus, the CSAO must constantly ask the question, "What is the specific finality of the athletic program on my campus?" When one considers how proportionately few students actually play varsity sports, it is no wonder that hard questions are being asked, especially when intercollegiate athletic programs are fueled by thousands and sometimes millions of dollars. The CSAO should strive to return feelings and humanity to athletics in a manner that is reasonable, respectable, educational, and developmental. Meaningful standards, both quantitative and qualitative, can be set for athletics, and the CSAO should be the key change agent in this process.

As Leonard (1975) so astutely states, there has been a split between mind, body, and spirit. The ideal unity of the intellectual, physical, and spiritual domains has been lost on far too many campuses. Athletes and intellectuals often live in different worlds, to the detriment of all. This split can and should be repaired by CSAOs who have the capability, authority, and responsibility to do so.

In addition, the CSAO must endeavor to balance the blatant institutional overemphasis on winning. Winning has become an absolute and a way of life in intercollegiate athletics, blinding us to other possibilities. Under these circumstances, the worst aspects of commercialism and professionalism threaten the balance of the mind, body, and spirit that a true student-athlete needs. Under heavy pressure for immediate victory, short-term excitement and intensity created by the overblown desire to win at all costs can, and frequently does, hurt the athlete in a deep, depressing, and long-term manner. The CSAO can help replace this situation with a new spirit that springs from the heart of the athletic experience itself — a spirit that is durable and meaningful.

References

Blake, E. S. "Classroom and Context: An Educational Dialect." *Academe,* September 1979, 280–292.

Golden, D. C. "Player Evaluation of Coaches." *American Football Coaches Association,* summer manual, 1980, 99–100.

Leonard, G. *The Ultimate Athlete: Revisioning Sports, Physical Education, and the Body.* New York: The Viking Press, 1975.

Michener, J. A. *Sports in America.* New York: Random House, 1976.

Dennis C. Golden is vice-president for student life at Duquesne University, Pittsburgh, Pennsylvania. He has also served as a guest lecturer and consultant in the field of student development and athletics. In addition, he has been a player and coach on the collegiate level, and has had experience as a professional athlete.

*College athletic programs are in danger of losing their
educational credibility, and their survival depends on
the unified intervention of concerned college administrators.*

College Sports:
Decisions for Survival

Joseph C. Mihalich

In a critique of college sports in *The Saturday Evening Post,* Stagg (1925)
said that the blame for the evils of the game "lies squarely on the door-
step of the faculties (who) are too superior to concern themselves with
such juvenile things." For millions of participants and spectators, college sports are the most popular expression of the sporting spirit, but
now, even more than in 1925, clouds of controversy shroud the October
afternoons and the race for national championships. Much has been
written about professionalism in college athletics, and there are disturbing reports of academic abuses in some institutions designed to
guarantee athletic eligibility at the price of education. In the wake of
such publicity, an increasingly critical public wonders about the role
and the value of athletics in higher education.

    The issue is critical for everyone involved, and especially critical
for administrators and faculty whose professional mandate is to safe-

Some material in this chapter is excerpted from the author's *Sports and Athletics:
Philosophy in Action,* Littlefield, Adams, Totowa, N.J. A version of this chapter will
appear in his forthcoming *Sports in the American Mind: Views and Perspectives,* Human
Kinetics Publishers, Champaign, Ill.

A. Shriberg, F. R. Brodzinski (Eds.). *Rethinking Services for College Athletes.* New Directions
for Student Services, no. 28. San Francisco: Jossey-Bass, December 1984.

71

guard integrity and probity in colleges and universities. To put it bluntly, college athletic programs are in danger of losing their educational credibility, and their survival depends on the unified intervention of concerned college administrators. The issue is that only academicians can define and defend the parameters of intercollegiate athletic programs, and that their failure to do so jeopardizes sports and athletics as a meaningful component in the educational process. Academicians are responsible as individuals and as institutional representatives for the moral character of college sports and the ethics of student participation.

In the tradition of meaningful education, properly conducted athletic programs are essential in sociocultural development at every level, including higher education. Beyond the lessons in self-descipline and self-motivation for student-athletes, beyond the impact of athletic programs on student bodies and loyal (contributing) alumni, the rationale for college sports reduces to the need to educate the total person in the pursuit of human excellence. From the days of the ancient Greeks, with their love of wisdom incarnated in physical beauty, to the message in Thomas Arnold's Rugby College, and to our own Presidential Councils on Physical Fitness, the adage is always the same: We need to educate both minds and bodies in the achievement of intellectual and physical excellence.

College Sports and Big Business

Intercollegiate sports and athletics have become big business. The socioeconomic dimension has come to rule here just as it rules the rest of the sporting enterprise and even society itself. Major college programs have multimillion dollar athletic budgets, and institutional revenue from winning programs totals hundreds of thousands of dollars from television contracts and post-season championship tournaments. The lure of such financial windfalls fuels the win-at-any-cost syndrome reflected in contemporary sports and society at large. Winning is important and lucrative in our competitive society, and some institutions do what must be done to guarantee sports dynasties with a realistic chance to place well in national championships. This means recruiting and retaining gifted athletes with little regard for academic ability and realistic academic progress. Reports of academic abuses include admitting athletes with unreasonably low entrance credentials — the equivalent of zero on Scholastic Aptitude Test (SAT) scores — falsifying academic records and mandating flimsy academic programs for student-athletes.

Such incidents tend to be limited to larger revenue-producing National Collegiate Athletic Association (NCAA) Division I football and basketball programs, and the entire issue must be kept in proper perspective. The vast majority of colleges and universities in the nation have priorities properly ordered, and maintain a proper balance between athletics and academics. In many institutions with modest athletic ambitions, the athletic program struggles to break even financially and in many cases it is a losing proposition. But the dream is always there, and many alumni hope that the athletic program will get bigger and better (and contribute accordingly). But the teams in the bowl games and other championships constitute the public image of college athletics, and the innocent institutions are implicated with the overly competitive minority.

How It All Happened

Like the greening of America and the making of the president, the professionalizing of college athletics reflects the efforts of diverse participants and interests. It all began innocently enough in the late nineteenth century when alumni from some of the most prestigious colleges and universities used the growing popularity of football to publicize their institutions and attract gifted students and faculty. Alumni involvement continued and intensified through the years, but the original intention of attracting gifted students and teachers changed to attracting gifted athletes. Colleges and universities derive much of their character and image from alumni contributions (financial and otherwise), and much of the pressure on college administrators comes from alumni who want their schools to become nationally visible through winning sports teams.

Alumni groups are only microcosms of the American social institution, an avid sports culture with a love for the competitive spirit expressed in the sporting experience. In return for our dedication and material support, we want our athletic programs to be just what they are — intensely competitive, professionally entertaining, and constantly available. The pragmatic explanation for the professionalizing of college sports is that millions of people are willing to pay millions of dollars to make it happen. Michener (1976) says that the professionalizing of college sports is a "fait accompli" and adds, "I would wish to hear no complaint that 'things oughtn't to be this way in a self-respecting institution of higher learning,' because they are that way and our society intends that they remain that way" (pp. 246–247).

Despite these incriminations, it is incongruous to charge the amorphous sociocultural institution with such specific actions as the professionalizing of college sports, and so the question becomes, "Who speaks for society in this area?" The answer is that national sports governing bodies and regional conferences are the link between society and our image of college athletics, and the most important of these is the NCAA, the national governing body for collegiate men's sports, and now, since the demise of the Association for Intercollegiate Athletics for Women, the sponsor of postseason championships for women's sports as well.

Colleges and universities must abide by NCAA regulations and recommendations, but this is a two-way street—the NCAA and the regional conferences must legislate wisely and effectively for the good of college sports. This raises the question, What is good for college sports and what do we want from our athletic programs? If what is good and what we want is intense competition and financial prosperity for winning teams (shared to some extent by all NCAA member institutions), then the NCAA is doing a good job. But if we want a better balance between academics and athletics, then we have cause to wonder about the present situation.

NCAA administrators will quickly point out that the association is comprised of representatives from the 930-odd member schools, and only speaks with their voice in determining policies and programs. This is true enough, but the NCAA is similar to other large organizations in that it contains power groups that may or may not represent the entire constituency to the constituency's satisfaction. These include major football and basketball schools, tournament selection committees responsible for choosing and ranking championship teams, the enforcement committee to investigate and penalize rules violations, and various internal committees including the prestigious Executive Council. There is no suggestion that any of these groups operate capriciously, but they do operate with sovereign powers, and special interests are frequently involved.

The sense of all this is that reform-minded college administrators need not tilt at windmills—their adversaries are highly visible and sometimes the adversary is us. Concerned college administrators must confront enthusiastic alumni who are willing to pay any price to make their schools nationally visible through sports. They must confront society at large—a society hooked on sports and willing to equate the sporting experience with the values of the ages. And they must confront sports governing bodies that have perhaps been influenced by the national euphoria over bowl games and other championships. But they must confront them, since this is the key to survival.

Reforms That Won't Work

Most popular proposals for reforms in college sports fall into three categories: reforms that would do more harm than good, reforms that discriminate against established groups in the college scene, and reforms that are really "Band-Aid" solutions to substantive problems. These categories are exemplified in recent proposals from a variety of sources.

Reforms That Self-Destruct. Some proposals recommend that we confront the obvious and legitimize professionalism in college sports. This approach advocates an honest separation between academics and athletics, and contends that college athletes should minimize their academic involvement and devote their time and energy to sports as paid professionals. This would eliminate the current hypocrisy that student-athletes are essentially students rather than athletes. Michener (1976) proposes that athletes in nationally competitive programs should be salaried as professional hires, and should be limited to taking one academic course in the semesters they compete in their sport. A fifth year of education would be included in the athletic grant to complete course requirements. Institutions with less ambitious athletic programs could scale down athletic involvement and increase academic progress.

Stevens (1980) recommends that certain colleges and universities should be designated as state-funded training centers for athletes, operated on a year-round basis to prepare professional football players as efficiently as possible. According to Stevens, "Trainees will not enroll in academic programs (and) their pay will be the same as that of assistant professors at the University of California" (p. 14). The sequel is a state-funded trust to underwrite a college education for the participants after their retirement from professional football.

These and similar plans are tempting to consider on a pragmatic basis, but they involve a sociocultural capitulation that we simply cannot afford. Our sociocultural morality is based on certain givens by which we live and act, and one of the most important is the integrity of the college experience. The question of right and wrong is paramount: It is one thing to recognize the existence of error, but quite another thing to want to build on fallacies to improve the situation. If professionalizing college sports is wrong—and it is—then we can gain nothing by making them more professional.

Reforms That Discriminate. Some reform proposals seek to advance the cause of college athletics at the expense of established components in the college scene. A good example is legislation known as Rule 48, enacted at the 1983 NCAA convention for implementation in

1986. Rule 48 requires that incoming student-athletes at Division I schools must score a minimum of 700 (total) on the SAT and have at least a 2.0 grade point average (G.P.A.) in a high school curriculum with required courses in English, mathematics, and the physical and social sciences. Rule 48 is intended to improve academic standards for student-athletes, and this is laudable, but the provisions of the legislation are discriminatory in several respects.

The most immediate negative reaction came from administrators at predominantly black colleges and universities, who argued that Rule 48 is discriminatory to black student-athletes. They point out that black applicants (athletes and nonathletes) historically score much lower on the SAT compared to white applicants. Recent studies confirm that black applicants scored an average of 220 points lower than white applicants in 1982, and the discrepancy is even greater in the previous six years covered in the study. The most telling statistic is that the national average for black students is 707 — only seven points higher than the 700-point minimum required by Rule 48 (*Chronicle of Higher Education*, 1983).

Rule 48's requirement of a high school G.P.A. of 2.0 in required subjects is also vulnerable, primarily because G.P.A.s cannot be measured equally among educationally diverse schools: a 2.0 in an elite prep school does not have the same meaning as a 2.0 in an inner-city school. Students in more privileged institutions are expected to attain a higher G.P.A. in all subjects, while a 2.0 in less privileged schools is often a superior attainment. This might be argued by administrators and faculty in inner city institutions, but there is enough discrepancy to make the 2.0 requirement debatable if not meaningless.

In a wider attack on Rule 48, critics contend that potential discrimination extends beyond racial and ethnic factors, and involves student-athletes in general compared to nonathlete students. Entrance requirements — including SAT scores — should be applied consistently to all incoming freshmen whether or not they participate in athletics. Colleges and universities are still free to admit whomever they will, but freshmen can compete in varsity sports only if they have the 700 board scores and the 2.0 G.P.A. This effectively constitutes an admissions policy, since athletic recruiters are likely to pass over high school prospects who do not measure up to Rule 48.

Probably the most substantive criticism of Rule 48 relates to the very nature of psychological testing to determine college success, and the intrinsic validity of SAT tests as an important factor in college admissions. Professional educators and competent observers wonder whether the SAT is structurally and ideologically sound as a psycho-

metric instrument, whether the SAT or any form of standardized testing can be reasonably accurate about any student's potential for success, whether the SAT is biased in favor of privileged social classes at
the expense of social minorities, and whether high school G.P.A.s are
really better predictors of college success than the SAT. (This analysis
of Rule 48 was written in collaboration with Lawrence Atkins, Temple
University School of Law.)

   Reforms That Miss the Point. Other reform proposals focus on
symptoms and incidentals rather than causes and substantive issues.
This is exemplified in periodic attempts to restore the freshman ineligibility rule in intercollegiate athletic programs. In the history of college
sports until the last decade, the freshman ineligibility rule was a respected
tradition in colleges and universities. The rule was intended to spare
freshmen the pressures of varsity competition while they adjusted to the
demands of college academics and athletics. In response to increasingly
competitive programs and the growing popularity of intercollegiate
athletics, the NCAA repealed the ineligibility rule beginning with the
1972–73 seasons. Some academic administrators argue for restoration
of the rule on the grounds that the original rationale still prevails, while
others (especially athletic directors) feel locked into the use of freshmen
by the demands and economies of major sports programs.

   In the nature of today's college scene, it is to everyone's advantage to let freshmen play. The rule against freshman eligibility is as
much of an anachronism as leather helmets, two-hand set shots, and
the innocence of lost generations. There was once a time and a reason
for the rule, but now the time has passed and the rule is no longer
viable. It was once probably true that most freshmen (athletes and nonathletes) needed at least a year to adjust to college, but now the college
experience for many is simply not that new or that different. Most
incoming freshmen today can anticipate what college will be like and
how they should respond.

   This is by no means true for all freshmen, nor is it easy or auto-
matic. There will always be some who need time to adjust—and some
never adjust to everyone's satisfaction. Although many college aspi-
rants today know what to expect in entering college, the experience still
requires effort and commitment to translate the expectation into reality. As in every human situation where theory and practice must combine, it is the individual student who must make it all work, and it is
typically human that some do this better than others.

   Times have changed for most incoming freshmen for several
reasons. There is (1) a more sophisticated social consciousness born of
earlier exposure to competitive life situations, (2) a greater familiarity

with the college experience derived from family and friends who have attended college in greater numbers than in the past, (3) an early anticipation and conscious preparation to attend college as the normal thing to do, (4) carefully designed college orientation programs at the high school and college entrance levels, and (5) an unprecedented level of technical preparation in sophisticated high school (and even grade school) athletic programs.

These factors vary among social and economic components in society, and have a longer history in privileged classes and affluent families. Some racial and ethnic minorities have yet to realize the full impact, but even here the awareness is felt and the gap is closing. This new awareness, and new opportunities in such groups, are due in no small part to athletic grants-in-aid for sons and daughters that frequently break the college barrier in minority families. Our competitive college sports programs sow the seeds of their own discontent, but a laudable aspect is the opportunity for so many minority student-athletes to be the first in their families to attend college.

The most significant problem for freshman student-athletes is the same problem that plagues athletes in advanced classes — finding the time and energy to serve the twin masters of academics and athletics. It can be handled with the proper budgeting of time and energy and with good peer role models to follow. Despite the new demands of college life, freshman athletes have an advantage since they have not yet learned the bad habits that doom some upperclassmen.

In the broad context of college athletics, the freshman eligibility controversy is merely an aspect of a larger situation that needs direction and control. The issue is simply a symptom of the intensely competitive character of college sports today. We need to restore sanity and perspective and a sense of proportion in our programs, and this is the responsibility primarily of academic administrators and boards of trustees. In Nietzsche's phrase, they must bring about a "transvaluation of values" to guarantee institutional priorities rather than overemphasis on sports for financial reasons. Freshman eligibility (or ineligibility) will cease to be an issue when college athletics again serve the purposes for which they are intended. In the meantime, nobody loses by letting freshmen play.

What We Need to Do

First of all, we must not panic. We need to recognize that the negative image of college sports is the result of highly publicized incidents at relatively few institutions. These institutions are nationally known because of their success in sports, and the public assumes that all colleges and universities operate in the same way for the same purposes. The vast majority of colleges and universities conduct ethllically sound and properly oriented athletic programs, and student-athletes in most schools compare favorably with nonathletes as serious and capable students. Reports of academic irregularities invariably involve a percentage of Division I schools with national championship aspirations, a fact that tacitly exonerates many schools in this division with Division II and III schools and National Association of Intercollegiate Athletics institutions. Most of these are colleges and universities with modest athletic ambitions (regional rather than national championships), and many base athletic grants-in-aid on financial need alone rather than athletic ability.

These tempering comments are by no means intended to minimize the problem of academic abuses or condone such practices in any way. This is a matter of principle and not numbers — even a few such transgressions are odious in view of the sacred mandate of institutions of higher learning. And it must be accepted that the financial rewards of athletic success are a constant temptation to develop nationally competitive programs by whatever means possible. We need to establish a climate of constructive renewal in which we can combine the values of athletic participation with the traditional purposes of higher education. Some critics would take the quick and easy way and eliminate or drastically de-emphasize college sports, but this would be a serious loss for society and would vitiate the education of the total person. Especially in our American society, we have come to appreciate the humanistic values of sports more than we ever have, and it would be self-defeating to negate this progress and deny ourselves the joy of sports.

Failures in the System. In the broad context of American education, we must confront some disturbing facts before we can evaluate college academics and college sports. Reports of academic irregularities involving student-athletes reveal a shocking lack of educational preparation prior to college entrance tests and college courses. This includes the inability to read or write at levels anywhere near college expectations. Many athletes — and nonathletes — struggle with SAT tests and academic programs simply because their educational progress was unrealistic at the elementary and secondary school levels. Among other things, they are the beneficiaries (or the victims) of the social promotion philosophy so popular in too many schools in recent years. Poor entrance scores and inferior academic performances are frequently the result of poor technical training rather than poor intellectual ability.

Many of us who labor in college classrooms have noticed a decline in the basic skills of many incoming freshmen — especially in reading comprehension and writing ability. Perhaps because of these deficiencies, there seems to be a lack of intellectual curiosity and no real desire to learn. This attitude is consistent with our sociocultural emphasis on vocational and pre-professional training for the job market rather than education for its own sake. The result is a stagnant educational system which has finally become an issue of national concern with high government priority. Attention at all levels, from the White House to concerned parents, is leading us to realize once again the importance of a liberal education to complement our pragmatic efficiency in socioeconomic affairs. Colleges and universities must be judicious in admitting and retaining marginal students (athletes and nonathletes), but our elementary and secondary schools must share the responsibility with our secular society.

Decisions for Survival. In a good example of the past as prologue, the most significant historical reform in college sports was the formation of the NCAA in 1904 at the request of President Theodore Roosevelt. In an effort to curb mounting violence in college football, Roosevelt ordered college presidents to band together to monitor college athletics — or else have them monitored by government control. The President bypassed athletic directors and appealed directly to college presidents to put their houses in order. The NCAA thus began as an organization of college presidents, and the academicians' gradual defection over the years is an operative factor in the troubled status of college sports. By the same token, the brightest hope for the future is the presence and active participation of so many college presidents at NCAA national conventions in the past few years. The most significant result is the passage of Rule 36 at the 1984 convention, which provides for a standing committee of forty-four college presidents empowered to make policy recommendations to the NCAA Executive Council.

This is the crux of the great reformation we need to restore sanity and perspective in college athletics. The only effective channels for realistic reform are college administrators working with sports governing bodies to enact and enforce constructive legislation. We need college presidents who are willing to resist the win-at-any-cost syndrome, to put their own houses in order first, and to guarantee an ethical climate and motivational support for balanced academic achievement and athletic participation. Morality in college athletics — like morality everywhere — cannot be legislated by the NCAA or any governing body. Moral issues and moral reforms are more fundamental than legislative directives, and must begin in the moral goodwill of the people involved. The ball is in the presidents' court, and they cannot afford to dribble it away for the second time since 1904.

It is easy enough to assign this weighty responsibility to college administrators — and for them to accept it — but the principles involved and techniques for implementation must be delineated. The noblest educational ideals are futile without systems of practical application and means to measure outcomes and goals. The principles are easily stated: First, sports and athletics are essential in the education of the total person and the achievement of excellence, and second, colleges and universities are obligated to provide an ethical climate and motivational support for balanced academics and athletics. These principles underlie the essentials of institutional responsibility for college athletic programs:

- The need to recognize and emphasize the dual role of student-athletes as students as well as athletes
- the need to restrict privileges for student-athletes to NCAA and conference regulations, and to what is available in principle to all students
- the need to recognize the mutually beneficial character of the institution's contractual agreement with student-athletes
- the need to recognize in a reasonable way the unique physical and psychological pressures and time and energy demands on student-athletes.

While the primary responsibility for the integrity of college athletics rests with presidents and academic administrators, the practical implementation of academic policy should be the province of professional academic athletic advisers. This is an emerging new breed of specialists who represent an important dimension in the future of college sports. Academic athletic advisers are usually academicians with professional expertise in student guidance and counseling and a constructive interest in the total college experience of the student-athlete. They function as liaison personnel between the academic adminstration and the nuts-and-bolts world of academic progress and timely graduation for student-athletes.

Academic athletic advisers achieved professional acceptance and national solidarity with the founding in 1976 of the National Association of Academic Athletic Advisors (NAAAA), an organization dedicated to developing professional attitudes and techniques to meet the special needs of advisement for college athletes. When all the sophisticated philosophies and policies of college athletics are in place, these are the people in the trenches who make everything work, who have the juggler's task of representing the administration honestly and fairly and serving as mentors and motivators and friends to student-athletes trying to succeed in the classroom and on the playing fields. They might well provide the critical missing link in reconciling academics and athletics.

Recommendations

These decisions for survival reduce to the following specific recommendations:

Go with the Times. Sociocultural phenomena such as college sports must be judged in the context of the society and culture in which they exist. Ours is an intensely competitive society where success is commonly measured in monetary terms. We must deplore excessive competition and exorbitant financial returns, but there is nothing wrong with healthy competition in sports and in life and suitable rewards in a society that is measured by such rewards. We will gain nothing by destroying our competitive spirit and eliminating reasonable incentives commensurate with accepted standards in our society. Our American culture is founded on the principles of competition and reward, and in suitable proportion these are contributory factors in the achievement of excellence. With intelligent direction and a sense of moderation, our college athletic programs can continue to be honestly competitive, reasonably rewarding, and academically sound.

Bring the Twain Together. One of the simplest mechanisms for improving college sports is a better relationship between academicians and athletic personnel. Since student-athletes are both students and athletes, it is essential that both faculty members and coaches should care and should share responsibility for the well-being of college athletes. Too many administrators and faculty members have no real consciousness of individuals in the sports complexes, and too many athletic directors and coaches have no real consciousness of individuals in the halls of learning. Both components must develop mutual respect and trust, and be willing to exchange views on purposes and goals. They must be mutually supportive of academics and athletics as institutional policies with legitimate values in the total college experience. College presidents should insist on such a relationship as an expression of institutional loyalty.

Appoint Academic Athletic Advisers. As indicated in earlier remarks, professionally trained academic athletic advisers are the key to the practical success of college athletic programs. Academic athletic advisers should be administrators or faculty members with stature and prestige on campus and access to all pertinent areas of academic and athletic administration. They should report directly to the president or an academic vice-president, and their salary should be budgeted by an academic department. In the institutional chain of command, they should not be subordinate to the athletic director and should not be paid by the athletic department. A possible exception to this rule involves newer associate and assistant athletic directors, many of whom have completed academic degrees in guidance and counseling and have practical experience in the field.

Five-Year Programs for Student-Athletes. College presidents would be wise to mandate five-year academic programs for student-athletes in nationally competitive programs, and to recommend five-year programs for student-athletes in less competitive programs. Athletic eligibility would remain at four years, and athletic grants-in-aid (if applicable) would be extended to cover the five-year educational program. This would ease pressure on college athletes by allowing them to take fewer than the normal five courses each semester (but certainly more than the one course that Michener suggests). In today's college milieu, many nonathlete students extend their college career for travel or work experience or even religious missions such as the Mormon apostolate at Brigham Young University. For many student-athletes, the elimination of one course each semester frequently enables them to cope much better with their academic schedules. For many athletes and nonathletes, the extra time could also accommodate remedial reading and writing courses to make the rest of their curriculum easier and more productive.

Involve the President. As indicated in earlier remarks, the NCAA's recently adopted Rule 36 empowers a group of forty-four college presidents to make policy recommendations to the Executive Council. Their involvement is invaluable, and their authority and expertise should be used flexibly and extensively. A worthy project would be a blue-ribbon Presidents Committee to answer the critical question, What is good for college sports and what do we want from our college programs? Let them evaluate education and athletics in every respect and concern — from college preparation programs to entrance requirements and graduation rates, from athletic grants-in-aid to tutorial services and faculty bias, and from independent television contracts to championship tournaments that make money but infringe on class attendance. Let them initiate a ten-year plan to correct excesses and defects and to restore misplaced integrity and let them guarantee the future of college sports as an enterprise of excellence. All this has been attempted before in various ways, but never by a panel with such power and prestige and such a vested interest in higher education.

References

The Chronicle of Higher Education, January 1983.

Michener, J. A. *Sports in America.* New York: Random House, 1975.

Stagg, A. A. *The Saturday Evening Post,* 1925.

Stevens, J. M. "How to Train and Education Professional Football Players." *Phi Delta Kappan,* September 1980.

Joseph C. Mihalich is professor of philosophy at La Salle College in Philadelphia, where he teaches a popular course in the philosophy of sports. He has served as a faculty delegate at NCAA national conventions, and is a member of the Philosophic Society for the Study of Sport, and the National Association of Academic Advisors for Athletes. He is the author of Sports and Athletics: Philosophy in Action *(1982) and the forthcoming* Sports in the American Mind: Views and Perspectives.

Further sources of information, including associations and publications, are listed in this chapter.

Sources of Additional Assistance

Arthur Shriberg, Sally E. Watson, Frederick R. Brodzinski

Associations

The following professional associations are only a sampling of the expanding number of groups formed to represent special issues, interests, and concerns in the world of college student athletes:

College Sports Information Directors of America (CoSIDA)
Contact: Fred Nuesch
                Sports Information Director
                Texas A & I University
                Kingsville, TX 78363
                (512) 592-0389

National Association of Collegiate Directors of Athletics (NACDA)
Contact: Michael J. Cleary
                Executive Director, NACDA
                1229 Smith Court, P.O. Box 16428
                Cleveland, OH 44116
                (216) 331-5773

Founded in the mid 1960s, NACDA was established to provide a means for college directors of athletics to share information, to provide

A. Shriberg, F. R. Brodzinski (Eds.). *Rethinking Services for College Athletes.* New Directions for Student Services, no. 28. San Francisco: Jossey-Bass, December 1984.

management training experiences, and to explore opportunities for athletic administrators to discover how they may better serve students and the college community. *Athletic Administration* is published by NACDA six times a year and focuses on trends in education and sports management. Its annual convention includes a business meeting and educational presentations on current topics of interest to approximately 2,000 members. An intensive annual management seminar follows the convention and includes state-of-the-art techniques for athletic administrators.

National Collegiate Athletic Association (NCAA)
    Nall Avenue at 63rd Street, P.O. Box 1906
    Mission, KS 66201

Officially convened in 1906, the NCAA speaks with the loudest and most authoritative voice for amateur athletics. Rules and regulations concerning athletics can be found in the *Manual of the National Collegiate Athletic Association,* published by the NCAA. The NCAA also provides representatives, available by telephone, to respond to inquiries, problems, and concerns.

National Intramural Recreational Sports Association (NIRSA)
Contact: Don C. Bailey
    Recreational Sports, 205 PEB
    North Texas State University
    Denton, TX 76203
    (817) 565-2275

This active organization is helpful to any campus seeking to develop intramural or recreation programs.

National Junior College Athletic Association (NJCAA)
    P.O. Box 1586
    Hutchinson, KS 67504

This organization coordinates most intercollegiate activities at the junior college level.

Women's Basketball Coaches of America (WBCA)
Contact: Betty Jaynes
    Suite 118, 150 Strafford Ave.
    Wayne, PA 19086

Further Readings

These writings provide information and lively discussion of the issues relating to student-athletes:

Hanford, H. "Controversies in College Sports." *Educational Record,* 1979, *60* (4), 351–366.

Mihalich, J. *Sports and Athletics: Philosophy in Action.* Totowa, N.J.: Littlefield, Adams, 1982.

Mihalich, J. *Sports in the American Mind: Views and Perspectives.* Champaign, Ill.: Human Kinetics, in press.

Oglesby, C. *Women in Sports: From Myth to Reality.* Philadelphia: Lea and Febiger, 1978.

Postow, B. C. (Ed.). *Women, Philosophy, and Sports.* Metuchen, N.J.: Scarecrow, 1983.

Purdy, E., Eitzen, D. S., and Hufnagel, R. "Are Athletes Also Students? The Educational Attainment of College Athletes." *Social Problems,* 1982, *29* (4), 439–448.

Schubert, G. W., and Schubert, A. F. "A Trilogy of Academic Concerns for the Advisor of Student Athletes: General Advising, Litigation, and NCAA Proposal Number 48." *NACDA Journal,* 1983, *3,* 11–22.

Sowa, C. J., and Gressard, C. F. "Athletic Participation: Its Relationship to Student Development." *Journal of College Student Personnel,* 1983, *24* (3), 236–239.

Vance, N. S. "Sport Is a Religion in America, Controversial Professor Argues." *Chronicle of Higher Education,* 1984, *24* (12), 25–28.

Welch, H., Jr. "The Exploitation of the Black Athlete: A Proposal for Change." *NASPA Journal,* 1982, *19* (3), 10–14.

Publications

Chronicle of Higher Education
1333 New Hampshire Ave., N.W.
Washington, DC 20036

Published weekly, this source for news in higher education devotes a section of its pages to athletics. Stories feature current trends in collegiate sports, NCAA actions, research, innovations, updates on continuing issues, administration, and many other topics of interest. In addition, the section features a sports calendar of upcoming meetings and championships and a section tracing promotions, job changes, and retirements of individuals in coaching and administration.

NCAA News
National Collegiate Athletic Association
P.O. Box 1906
Mission, KS 66201

This official weekly publication of the NCAA covers athletics, athletes, coaches, and events, and publishes rule interpretations, championship dates and sites, position announcements, statistics, sporting results, controversies, and general items of interest and importance. The *NCAA News* reports activities in NCAA Divisions I, II, and III.

Newspapers. Your local sports pages can provide a wealth of information on local, regional, and national levels. Standings, statistics, and articles of interest are featured. *U.S.A. Today* provides a concise daily summary of nationwide sports information.

Athletic Administration
NACDA
1229 Smith Court, P.O. Box 16428
Cleveland, OH 44116
(216) 331-5773

The official publication of the National Association of Collegiate Directors of Athletics.

Report of the Select Committee on Athletic Problems and Concerns in Higher Education. NCAA, April 1985.

Popular Media. Articles about intercollegiate athletics are in vogue and can be found in many popular magazines.

Also of Interest

There are approximately fifty sports administration programs at various colleges and universities around the country. Ten years ago, there were only a handful of programs, and their swift proliferation has created some problems. The earliest programs, and most of those that followed, were based, physically and philosophically, in the physical education department. The best programs today, those providing the most appropriate schedule of professional instruction, originate in the business division. These tend to focus on skills needed now and in the future for athletic administrators, including marketing, sports writing, administrative theory and practice, educational development, and public relations among other curriculum areas. Some of the best programs are located at Robert Morris College, Ohio University, and Biscayne College. Northeastern University has recently established an academic center called the Center for the Study of Sport in Society. It is directed by Richard Upchurch, North 360 Huntington Avenue, Boston, MA 02115. Facilities of this kind are starting to emerge on many campuses across the nation.

Arthur Shriberg is vice-president for student development at Xavier University in Cincinnati, Ohio, and vice president-elect of the American Association of University Administrators. He chairs a special task force of the American College Personnel Association on the proper role of intercollegiate athletics, and has supervised Division I, II, and III athletic programs at four college campuses.

Sally E. Watson is assistant to the vice-president for student development at Xavier University. She has been involved in the study of the needs of student-athletes on campuses in the Midwest and the South and through her activities in the American College Personnel Association.

Frederick R. Brodzinksi is dean of students at Ramapo College in New Jersey. He is active in several professional organizations and is a popular speaker at professional seminars across the country.

APPENDIX

Your Rights and Responsibilities as a Student-Athlete in Higher Education

James J. Rhatigan

Students considering participation in intercollegiate athletics need to give careful attention to choosing the college or university appropriate for them. You are such a person, and no doubt you will be concerned about the athletic facilities, team members, coaches, schedule, and the amount of "playing time" you can expect at institutions you are considering.

This brochure has been developed to call your attention to other matters of importance which may not be as familiar to you. Its purpose is to help you reach your goals by taking steps leading to a more informed choice of an institution, and to make you more aware of your rights and responsibilities as an enrolled student-athlete at the institution you select.

Several considerations are set forth in the brochure. These issues are found on all campuses, but the campuses do not handle them in the same way. This guide will help you ask the right questions; it will urge you to accept your responsibilities, and to insist on your rights.

It is up to you, of course, to evaluate the answers you receive. You may need help from your parents, guardian, or a high school counselor, teacher, coach, or athletic director, in sorting through the answers you receive from institutions in which you are interested. This brochure could reduce significantly the possibility of being surprised, disappointed, or frustrated in your choice of a school. It may also be helpful throughout your college years, so you may wish to keep it available.

Institutions want their student-athletes to succeed academically. It must be emphasized, however, that only by accepting responsibility for your choices can you protect your rights. You will be well served to ask the right questions now.

Admission

1. You are responsible for applying for admission to the institution of your choice, to supply a high school transcript, and to provide such additional information as the institution may require.

2. Most institutions of higher education now require an admissions test. The major tests are the American College Test (ACT) and the Scholastic Aptitude Test (SAT). It is your responsibility to find out if one of these standard tests is required at the institutions you are considering. If so, high school counselors will be able to advise you of the time and place the tests will be offered. If you feel the score you receive does not reflect your true ability, you have the right to take the test again. Again, counselors will advise you how to proceed.

3. Admissions standards vary significantly from institution to institution. If you are admitted to an institution, it is an indication of that school's assessment of your prospects to succeed academically. Some student-athletes with a history of academic problems are admitted as exceptions to these rules. Certainly there is nothing wrong in that, but it should signal to you that additional academic effort on your part may be required for you to succeed. Some schools have an "open admissions" policy, which means they are open to all high school graduates in the State (most open-admissions schools are State schools). This will require you to ask of your high school counselor or the academic counselors you should meet during a college visit, how your test scores compare to those of other enrolled students.

4. You may apply for admission to as many institutions as you wish. Acceptance at one or more institutions represents no commitment on your part to enroll. Just make sure you do not sign your name to any letter of intent or other document until you have decided which institution you want to attend. It is your responsibility — in consultation with parents or guardians — to make this choice. Be wary of persons using pressure tactics aimed at influencing your decison.

Making the Final Choice

1. You have a responsibility to be fully prepared for college work. In spite of this, some students do have one or more deficiencies in their level of preparation. You have the right in this instance to determine in advance whether an institution has courses or special programs to help students in your circumstance. You need to discuss openly your deficient academic areas with the coaches recruiting you. It will be helpful to inquire about the nature of the university's interest and/or ability to provide the academic assistance you may need; look for coaches who will make positive suggestions.

2. One way to get a feel for an institution's commitment to student-athletes is to look at the academic success rate of student-athletes. This can be a tough issue for schools to present, as students leave school for all kinds of reasons. While you don't want to be dazzled by statistics, give institutional representatives a chance to explain their student academic success rate with you. You should be wary of any institution which refuses to discuss this openly.

3. The vast majority of intercollegiate coaches care a great deal for the welfare of the student-athletes whom they have recruited. Nonetheless, you have a responsibility to yourself to look as closely as you can at those persons recruiting you. If you are invited to the campus for a visit you can learn much from other students. You will also receive some indication of the quality of a program by observing who you meet and what you learn about the institution during a visit.

4. Your responsibility as a student-athlete will require a significant amount of your time, energy, and concentration. You have a right to be informed of any support services the campus may provide to encourage your growth as an individual.

5. Once enrolled, some student-athletes realize the institution they chose does not meet their needs. Should you find yourself in this circumstance, you have every right to ask about how you may transfer to another institution, and to determine who will help in making this change possible for you. The transfer question is tricky so you will need help in learning what is involved.

Financial Assistance

1. Some athletes receive financial assistance for participating in an intercollegiate sport. If you are offered full or partial financial assistance for participating in a sport, you will want to be informed of and fully understand the factors which will result in your keeping or losing that aid during your enrollment. You have a right to expect those factors to be available to you in writing prior to enrollment. You also have the right to know who makes the decision on your aid, and what appeals are available should you feel

a decision affecting that aid has been unfairly made. It will be helpful to ask what costs you will have to pay out of your own pocket.

2. Some students in difficult economic circumstances will be entitled to Federal financial assistance in addition to an athletic grant — even if it is a full grant. You have the right to know the maximum amount of financial assistance for which you are eligible. This information can be obtained from any institution's Financial Aids Office.

3. Many institutions cannot make full grants-in-aid to all student athletes. Even in larger programs there are limits, especially in minor sports. Often an aid "package" using several sources of funds may be put together for you. Some of these "packages" require you to reapply annually. If a combination "package" is offered, it is your responsibility to adhere to annual application deadlines. The Financial Aids Office at any institution will have these dates available. These aid "packages" are entirely proper and legitimate. You just need to understand them. Your high school counselor or principal can be of help.

4. Some student-athletes assume that an athletic grant-in-aid is automatically renewed. In actuality, for NCAA, NJCAA, and NAIA institutions, the awards are made annually. In investigating your choice of an institution, you should inquire about the usual reasons for non-renewal.

5. Some students who do not receive an athletic grant may elect to be a "walk-on" and participate anyway. This decision is often made in the hope of receiving an athletic grant at some later point. If you are in this circumstance, it is your right to know at what level you must perform to be assured of receiving aid from the Athletic Department at some later point. Who will make this commitment to you? The answer may vary by institution, but you need to find out.

6. The time commitment for athletics at some institutions may make it difficult for some student-athletes to graduate in four years. If you come to realize at any time during your college career that you will have difficulty in completing your studies in four years, you have the right to ask about the institution's record in providing a fifth year of financial assistance, and the conditions that pertain to that assistance. It cannot be guaranteed for any student in advance. If the history exists in institutions for providing a fifth year of financial aid, you have the right to be informed of the nature and amount of this aid.

Some Academic Issues

1. As an enrolled student you have the right to receive guidance from an academic advisor, and to register an objection with your college dean if you feel you are not receiving helpful assistance. However, you are responsible for your own schedule and for taking courses leading toward a degree.

Some students are undecided about a major. You have the right to expect help in arriving at a decision, which may include career counseling. Academic advisors, professors, coaches, and other interested persons can also be sources of help.

If you consider yourself to be a high caliber athlete with aspirations for a career in professional sports, you should know that only a tiny percentage of student-athletes will achieve this goal. Be wise; seek help in choosing a major. Even those who do play professionally for a number of years need the education that was readily available during their collegiate experience. Some of these former student-athletes have commented on the mistakes they made. It is within your power to avoid these mistakes.

2. You may encounter personal problems in college that interfere with classwork. You have the right to know if personal counseling is provided by the campus you are considering.

3. You have the responsibility as an enrolled student to adhere to the academic rules and regulations established by the institution.

4. The greater athletic role you play, the harder it may be for you to achieve your full academic potential. This is particularly true in the "big-time," high-pressure sports. Achievement can be accomplished, but it will require extraordinary personal discipline.

5. You have a right to know whether the institution has a policy which permits special consideration in making up exams or missed work due to absences for team travel or other legitimate reasons beyond your control. If the institution has no policy, you have the right to expect that academic advisors will inform you of individual instructors who will or will not be of assistance in this context. Even when exceptions are made, you have the responsibility to complete the work expected of all students.

6. Your schedule during the year may make summer school enrollment desirable or necessary. You have the right to be informed of arrangements, if any, which will be made for you during the summer, including housing, a job, or other benefits an institution can legitimately provide.

Injury

1. Your participation in training programs, practice sessions, and intercollegiate competition carries the risk of injury. You have a right to know the exact medical benefits and treatment to which you are entitled should you become injured.

2. Should you experience an injury, you will be responsible for adherence to the program of rehabilitation prescribed. Following the healing of your injury you again will be responsible for participation in your sport. If you are concerned about the status of your recovery from injury, you have the right to refrain from any physical activity until all medical opinions concur on your recovery. You have the right to expect additional opinions should you be uncertain or dissatisfied with an original opinion.

3. If the injury you receive prohibits further athletic competition, you have the right to know whether the athletic grant you may be receiving will be continued — and for how long. This determination should be made before you decide to enroll at a specific institution, not after you sustain an injury.

4. Your participation in an intercollegiate sport carries with it the remote chance of catastrophic injury. You have the right to know what benefits the institution provides for catastrophic injury.

Conduct

1. Every institution has rules of conduct expected of students, though the rules differ among institutions. Whichever institution you select, the rules of conduct applying to all students also govern student-athletes.

2. In addition to the rules governing all students, coaches and/or Athletic Departments typically add team rules. These rules are important because they potentially affect your status as a student-athlete. It is considered a *privilege* rather than a *right* to be a student-athlete, and the privilege can be removed. You should ask to see a copy of team rules before enrolling at an institution.

3. While participating as a student-athlete, you have a right to expect team rules to be fairly and uniformly applied, and you should insist on your right to appeal any decision concerning alleged violations you consider to be unjust.

4. Your personal conduct as a student-athlete can be compared to that of public persons. Thus both your accomplishments and your personal failings may be observed and reported by the media. In the case of alleged off-campus misconduct, you have the right to know whether campus officials or Athletic Department officials will take action; if the institution does respond to off-campus misconduct, it is important for you to be informed of whether it will wait until the matter is resolved by the off-campus courts, agencies, or persons involved. You also have a right to be informed as to what help the Athletic Department or institution will provide you in preparing your statements for the media, in obtaining legal counsel, or in protecting you from the unwarranted invasion of your privacy.

5. The Federal Family Educational Rights and Privacy Act protects the confidentiality of your educational records. No information concerning your grades or any other educational matters can be released without your consent.

6. You do not leave your rights as a citizen at the door when you enter a university/college. Your familiarity with the basic rights of citizens is a responsibility you must assume as a protection against unwarranted behavior on the part of anyone in an institution.

Conclusion

By asking clear questions of institutions you should expect to receive clear answers. It is hoped that the above material will help you in this respect. Of course students will differ in the priority they give to issues; only you can decide what is important. Certainly you may have questions of importance not covered here; write them down and make them a part of the process you will use in selecting a college or university.

Index

U.S. POSTAL SERVICE

STATEMENT OF OWNERSHIP, MANAGEMENT AND CIRCULATION
(Required by 39 U.S.C. 3685)

1. TITLE OF PUBLICATION	A. PUBLICATION NO	2. DATE OF FILING
New Directions for Student Services	4 4 9 0 7 0	9/30/84

3. FREQUENCY OF ISSUE	A. NO. OF ISSUES PUBLISHED ANNUALLY	B. ANNUAL SUBSCRIPTION PRICE
quarterly	4	$35 inst/$25 indv

4. COMPLETE MAILING ADDRESS OF KNOWN OFFICE OF PUBLICATION *(Street, City, County, State and ZIP Code) (Not printers)*

433 California St., San Francisco (SF County), CA 94104

5. COMPLETE MAILING ADDRESS OF THE HEADQUARTERS OR GENERAL BUSINESS OFFICES OF THE PUBLISHERS *(Not printers)*

433 California St., San Francisco (SF County), CA 94104

6. FULL NAMES AND COMPLETE MAILING ADDRESS OF PUBLISHER, EDITOR, AND MANAGING EDITOR *(This item MUST NOT be blank)*

PUBLISHER *(Name and Complete Mailing Address)*

Jossey-Bass Inc., Publishers, 433 California St., S.F., CA 94104

EDITOR *(Name and Complete Mailing Address)*

Ursula Delworth, Gary Hanson, Univ. of Iowa, Iowa City, Iowa 52242

MANAGING EDITOR *(Name and Complete Mailing Address)*

Allen Jossey-Bass, Jossey-Bass Publishers, 433 California St., S.F., CA 94104

7. OWNER *(If owned by a corporation, its name and address must be stated and also immediately thereunder the names and addresses of stockholders owning or holding 1 percent or more of total amount of stock. If not owned by a corporation, the names and addresses of the individual owners must be given. If owned by a partnership or other unincorporated firm, its name and address, as well as that of each individual must be given. If the publication is published by a nonprofit organization, its name and address must be stated.) (Item must be completed)*

FULL NAME	COMPLETE MAILING ADDRESS
Jossey-Bass Inc., Publishers	433 California St., S.F., CA 94104

For names and addresses of stockholders, see attached list.

8. KNOWN BONDHOLDERS, MORTGAGEES, AND OTHER SECURITY HOLDERS OWNING OR HOLDING 1 PERCENT OR MORE OF TOTAL AMOUNT OF BONDS, MORTGAGES OR OTHER SECURITIES *(If there are none, so state)*

FULL NAME	COMPLETE MAILING ADDRESS
Same as #7	

9. FOR COMPLETION BY NONPROFIT ORGANIZATIONS AUTHORIZED TO MAIL AT SPECIAL RATES *(Section 411.3, DMM only)*
The purpose, function, and nonprofit status of this organization and the exempt status for Federal income tax purposes *(Check one)*

☐ (1) HAS NOT CHANGED DURING PRECEDING 12 MONTHS ☐ (2) HAS CHANGED DURING PRECEDING 12 MONTHS *(If changed, publisher must submit explanation of change with this statement.)*

10. EXTENT AND NATURE OF CIRCULATION	AVERAGE NO. COPIES EACH ISSUE DURING PRECEDING 12 MONTHS	ACTUAL NO. COPIES OF SINGLE ISSUE PUBLISHED NEAREST TO FILING DATE
A. TOTAL NO. COPIES *(Net Press Run)*	2610	2705
B. PAID CIRCULATION 1. SALES THROUGH DEALERS AND CARRIERS, STREET VENDORS AND COUNTER SALES	305	69
2. MAIL SUBSCRIPTION	837	875
C. TOTAL PAID CIRCULATION *(Sum of 10B1 and 10B2)*	1142	944
D. FREE DISTRIBUTION BY MAIL, CARRIER OR OTHER MEANS SAMPLES, COMPLIMENTARY, AND OTHER FREE COPIES	119	115
E. TOTAL DISTRIBUTION *(Sum of C and D)*	1261	1059
F. COPIES NOT DISTRIBUTED 1. OFFICE USE, LEFT OVER, UNACCOUNTED, SPOILED AFTER PRINTING	1349	1646
2. RETURN FROM NEWS AGENTS	0	0
G. TOTAL *(Sum of E, F1 and 2 - should equal net press run shown in A)*	2610	2705

11. I certify that the statements made by me above are correct and complete

SIGNATURE AND TITLE OF EDITOR, PUBLISHER, BUSINESS MANAGER, OR OWNER

John R. Ward   Vice-President

PS Form 3526 July 1981   *(See instruction on reverse)*   (Page 1)